Library of
Davidson College

Two Masters, One Message

Two Masters, One Message

Roy C. Amore

ABINGDON
NASHVILLE

Two Masters, One Message

Copyright © 1978 by Roy C. Amore

All rights reserved

No part of this book may be reproduced in any manner whatsoever without written permission of the publisher except brief quotations embodied in critical articles or reviews. For information address Abingdon, Nashville, Tennessee.

Library of Congress Cataloging in Publication Data

AMORE, ROY C   1942-
  Two masters, one message.

  1. Christianity and other religions—Buddhism. 2. Buddhism—Relations—Christianity. 3. Buddhism—Influence. I. Title.
BR128.B8A47   261.2   77-18062
ISBN 0-687-42750-9
ISBN 0-687-42751-7 pbk.

Scripture quotations unless otherwise noted are from the Revised Standard Version Common Bible, copyright © 1973 by the Division of Christian Education of the National Council of Churches.

MANUFACTURED BY THE PARTHENON PRESS AT
NASHVILLE, TENNESSEE, UNITED STATES OF AMERICA

This book is dedicated to the late Carl Michalson and Will Herberg of Drew University and to the other outstanding teachers who have shared their light with me.

CONTENTS

List of Abbreviations   9
Introduction   11

I. **Two Masters**   15
     How Masters Descend   15
     How Masters Live   30
     How Masters Return   45

II. **One Message**   58
     The Way to a Pure Mind   58
     Parables   80
     Miracles   85

III. **The Question of Borrowing**   96
     One Hundred Years of Scholarship on the Question   96
     How Buddhism Could Have Influenced the New Testament   106

IV. **A Case for Buddhist Influence**   137
     Q Is B: A Hypothesis   137
     Evidence Against the Hypothesis   165

Conclusion   177
     Appraisal of the Hypothesis   178
     Implications for the Historical Jesus   183

Notes   187
Bibliography   200
Index   202

LIST OF ABBREVIATIONS

Christian Gospels
  Mark   The Gospel According to Mark
  Matt.   The Gospel According to Matthew
  Luke   The Gospel According to Luke
  John   The Gospel According to John

Versions of the Buddhist Dharmapada
  GDh   *The Gāndhārī Dharmapada,* trans. from Gāndhārī by the author
  PDh (B)   *The Dhammapada,* trans. from Pali by Irving Babbitt
  PDh (R)   *The Dhammapada,* trans. from Pali by S. Radhakrishnan
  Uv   *Udanavarga,* trans. from Tibetan by W. W. Rockhill

Biographies of the Buddha
  Intro. Jat.   Introduction to the Jatakas (Nidāna-kathā), trans. from Pali by T. W. Rhys Davids in *Buddhist Birth Stories*
  Mv   *Mahāvastu,* trans. from Sanskrit by J. J. Jones

INTRODUCTION

One cannot read the Sermon on the Mount without feeling that it is an abridged version of parts of the Dhammapada.
Soma Thera, *The Contribution of Buddhism to World Culture*

The moral teaching of the Buddha has a remarkable resemblance to that of the Sermon on the Mount.
B. H. Streeter, *The Buddha and the Christ*

To love one's enemies, to bless them that curse, to do good to them that hate, to turn the other cheek, to leave the cloak with him who takes the coat, to give all to him who asks, which are the teachings of Jesus, are precepts not only taught but practised in their extreme rigour by the Buddha.
S. Radhakrishnan, *Eastern Religions and Western Thought*

    I am a Christian and have studied Christian thought in some detail, but my profession is to research and teach about other religions, especially Buddhism, for which I have a great deal of appreciation. In my research on Buddhism I have from time to time come across intriguing quotations such as the three cited above. In spite of the fact that it is well known that Buddhism is very different from the monotheist religions of the West such as Christianity, we have in the foregoing statements the opinion of a Buddhist, a Christian, and a Hindu scholar that the teachings of Gautama Buddha and Jesus Christ are quite comparable. A contemporary Zen Buddhist Master has said, "Jesus was a Zen Master." I know how difficult it is to earn the title Zen Master, so I wondered how it could be bestowed posthumously upon

Jesus. Curiosity triumphed, and I set aside a week for comparing the teaching of Jesus in the Sermon on the Mount with that of Gautama in the collection of Buddhist sayings known as the Dharmapada (pronounced dar-ma-pa-da). The comparison was so interesting and involved that I have spent four years on it.

My comparison began with just the two brief collections of sayings, the Sermon on the Mount and the Dharmapada; but soon I was led to compare other sayings of Jesus and Gautama, and from there the larger question of their similar life-styles arose. This in turn led to the observation that at some points the stories of the birth of Gautama and Jesus are strikingly similar. I now wish to share my findings with the reader.

Part one (the first two chapters) compares the life and teachings of Jesus and Gautama. I deal mainly with those Christian teachings which are similar to Buddhist teachings. This means passing over many matters about which Christians and Buddhists differ. Buddhism originated in northern India in the sixth century before Jesus, and it reflects the social institutions and ideological beliefs of that place and period. Christianity likewise reflects the social and ideological world view of some Jews who lived in an international environment around the Mediterranean Sea over five hundred years later. In spite of these vastly different cultural settings, however, there are several points at which the Buddhist and Christian traditions intersect.

Part two (chapters 3 and 4) deals with a question that arises from the comparisons of the first part: *Did one tradition borrow from the other?* Is that why there are so many similarities? In the last chapter I suggest an argument that seems to best fit the evidence, and in the Conclusion the relevance of the proposal for understanding the historical Jesus will be considered.

This book goes out on a scholarly limb, and some readers will not want to go all the way. At first the limb is fairly solid and broad, when I explore those teachings which Jesus and

Introduction

Gautama have in common and compare the similar stories that were told about the two masters. But later in the book the limb becomes more narrow and shaky, when I explore the possibility that some Buddhist sayings found their way into the New Testament in Christian guise.

Why should a scholar go out on such a limb? Because uncharted avenues of human thought call out like unexplored caves and unclimbed mountains. I am not the first to venture out this particular limb, for there were a few such adventurous scholars around the turn of the last century, as I shall recall in the third chapter. They did not fall off, nor were they pushed off by the weighty arguments by opponents. Rather they were largely ignored; yet the branch of human thought that they began to explore remains today. While most scholars and missionaries feature the many differences in the teachings of Jesus and Gautama, there is another side to the coin. A number of similar sayings dealing with themes of contemporary interest such as nonviolence and purity of mind may be found in the teachings attributed to the two great masters. Should we ignore these similarities and their implications? Certainly it is possible to ignore them. Christianity and Buddhism have coexisted on this planet and competed for followers for almost two millennia while going their separate ways, but I think an exploration of their similarities is of value to both Buddhists and Christians. We must not be like the person Stephen Leacock describes in *Sunshine Sketches of a Little Town.* When a person receives a Ph.D. degree, he writes, "he is pronounced full. No new ideas may be imparted to him."

The similarities in the teachings of the two masters and the stories of the two masters that I present in the first part of this book may be accounted for in a number of ways. To some the similarities will seem so general that they can be dismissed as mere coincidence. Others may argue that God inspires all true prophets to give essentially the same message, although the particulars are altered to suit the mentality of the prophet's particular era and audience. Or it may be that Jesus, Gautama, and some other great religious spokesmen were drawing upon a common core of wise sayings that have long existed among humans but that come fully to expression only rarely. One or more of these explanations may account for all the similarities between the teachings of the two masters, but there is another possibility. *It may be that one religion drew upon the wisdom of the other.* The second part of this book explores that possibility. It is a controversial area, and the conclusions are admittedly tentative. They may disturb some readers, but if so I pray that it will be like the productive disturbance that farmers must work upon the soil in the spring in order to harvest in the fall.

As I finish this manuscript the Thanksgiving holiday rapidly approaches, a festival that itself was influenced by the "Indian" spirituality that European Christians found in the Americas. So it seems especially appropriate to thank those who have directly helped me with this book about the relation of another Indian spirituality to the Christians of an earlier era. I gratefully acknowledge the many forms of help I have received in writing this book. Previous scholars such as Richard Garbe and Albert Edmunds made my work easier. Helpful editorial suggestions came from Larry Shinn and Bernard Cooke, and Gerry Bryant typed the manuscript with her usual speed and accuracy. Most of all, I wish to acknowledge the editorial contributions of Judy Amore.

I
TWO MASTERS

How Masters Descend

Comparable stories are told about the descent of Jesus and Gautama from the heavens. Many of the details in these Christian and Buddhist stories reflect an ancient, legendary pattern that may have served as their prototype. This pattern includes a description of the master's descent into the womb of a pure, female human who conceives the child without sexual intercourse. It includes an account of the master's birth and the honor that was paid to him by angels and prophets. There is little told about the childhood of the masters' lives, but the stories about their life-styles as adults are quite plentiful. Perhaps the most intriguing episodes tell of their spiritual quests and their struggles with the devil. Finally, the pattern includes an account of how the masters conquer death; though their physical bodies do die, they leave behind communities of disciples to carry on their missions.

Before considering the particular stories that are told about Gautama and Jesus, I wish to comment on the ancient pattern itself, upon the legendary theme that savior figures visit the earth from time to time to conquer evil and set up an era of righteousness. To accomplish such a mission they must first come down to earth from one of the heavenly regions or spheres. One Sanskrit word for this is *avatar* (avatāra), "down-coming," or "descent."

The idea that gods descend from the sky to earth is extremely old and common in the history of religions. For instance, in the story about the garden of Eden it is said that God comes to walk in the garden in the cool of the night. But in such accounts God visits earth in a spiritual body—the Hebrews are much more reluctant to describe this spiritual presence on earth than most other cultures, but they do speak of God manifest in clouds of mist, columns of fire, or a burning bush.

There is an alternative way of conceiving the visit of a god to earth. That way tells of the descent of the god into the womb of a human. I will call the latter motif "god in a human body," to distinguish it from the less material "god in a spiritual body."

God in a spiritual body. Most of the religious conceptions and patterns of worship employed by classical Hinduism and Buddhism date from before the sixth century B.C., when Gautama lived in the central part of northern India. Some of these background conceptions were brought to India by the Aryans, who, with horses and war chariots, overran northwest India several centuries before Gautama.

The Aryans in India believed in an intermediate space and an overarching sky filled with various gods and goddesses who occasionally appeared on earth when it suited their purposes. These gods appeared on earth in bodies that appeared to be human but in fact were spiritual.

The story of Dhamayanti, a princess who had fallen in love with Prince Nala, tells how four gods came to earth looking exactly like Nala. When the princess was to choose a husband from an assembly of royal hopefuls, she was astonished and vexed to see five Prince Nalas. She appealed to the gods to assume their proper god-bodies, and when they obliged she saw them in their spiritual bodies, which were "unwinking, with unwithered garlands and free from dust, standing without touching the ground." The verbs used to describe the motion of the gods-come-down in spiritual bodies are those appropriate to wind or lightning. The four gods "blow" from place to place, instantly, and they pass through the palace walls without difficulty.

Two Masters

The Buddhist texts often describe the appearance of a god on earth in similar terms, as the following quotation about the god Brahmā demonstrates:

> Then Brahmā Sahampati became aware in his mind of the thought in the Blessed One's mind, and as soon as a strong man might extend his flexed arm or flex his extended arm, he vanished in the Brahma-world and appeared before him. He arranged his upper robe on one shoulder, and raising his hands palms together towards the Blessed one, he said . . .[1]

From the same passage we learn how the deity ascends again to heaven: "And after he had paid homage to him, keeping him on his right, he vanished at once."

The pattern is clear; the old belief in India (and elsewhere) was that a god could instantly and effortlessly descend to earth, assume the shape and color of a material body, and could ascend again as quickly and mysteriously as he descended. This *spiritual* body is less physical than a *human* body but more physical than the heavenly bodies the gods assume when in their heavenly habitats.

God in a human body. Now I turn to the pattern of belief that emerged along the Ganges River and found its way into Buddhism and other Indian traditions. The earliest biography of a Buddha that exists in Buddhist literature[2] establishes the *pattern* for all Buddhas in all eras. The later stories of the birth and early life of Gautama, the Buddha for this era, may be seen as expansions upon this framework biography inherited from very early Buddhism or from pre-Gautama beliefs along the Ganges River. The text describes the stages through which all Buddhas have gone, from the time of their preexistence in a heaven to the time of their founding an order of disciples to teach the saving message for their era. It is important to note that all masters are thought to be born according to this pattern.[3]

1) The master "descended into his mother's womb mindful and self-possessed. That in such a case, is the rule."

2) At the time of the descent of the master, "there is made manifest throughout the universe . . . an infinite and splendid radiance, passing the glory of the gods. . . . That . . . is the rule."
3) At the time of the descent of the master, the four archangels go to the four quarters of the earth to protect him, saying, "Let no one . . . work harm to the Bodhisat or to the mother of the Bodhisat!" That . . . is the rule.
4) The mother of the master "is a woman virtuous through her own nature: averse from taking life, averse from taking what is not given, averse from unchastity, averse from lying speech, averse from indulgence in strong drinks. That . . . is the rule."
5) His mother remains chaste during the conception, while carrying the child and after giving birth, for his "mother has no mind for indulgence in the pleasures of sense with men, and is incapable of transgression with any man whatever who may be enamoured of her. That . . . is the rule."
6) At the time, the mother is completely happy, for all of her desires are satisfied. That . . . is the rule.
7) When she is carrying the baby in her womb, she experiences no discomfort and "within her womb she sees the Bodhisat complete in the endowment of all his organs and his limbs. That . . . is the rule."
8) "On the seventh day after the birth of a Bodhisat, the mother of the Bodhisat dies, and rises again in the heaven of Delight. That . . . is the rule."
9) Unlike many other women, the mother carries the baby exactly ten lunar months. That . . . is the rule.
10) "Whereas other women bring forth sitting or reclining, the mother of a Bodhisat brings forth not so, but standing. That . . . is the rule."
11) When the baby is born, the four archangels receive him first and worship him, saying, "Rejoice, lady, for Mighty is the son that is born to thee!" That . . . is the rule.
12) When the master is born, he comes forth "undefiled by any uncleanness whatever, pure, spotless. That . . . is the rule."
13) "Two showers of water appear from the sky, one of cold, the other of warm water, wherewith they do the needful bathing of the Bodhisat and of his mother. That . . . is the rule."
14) As soon as he is born the infant master "stands firm on both feet

and, with his face to the north, takes seven strides, the while a white canopy is held over him, and looking around on every side, he utters as with the voice of a bull: 'Chief am I in the world, Eldest am I in the world, Foremost am I in the world! This is the last birth! There is now no more coming to be!' That . . . is the rule."
15) At the time of the birth of the master, "an infinite and splendid radiance passing the glory of the gods appears throughout the world. That . . . is the rule."

The text continues with an account of the prophecies that the baby, endowed with the thirty-two marks of a superperson, would grow up to be either a great emperor if he chooses to live a layman's life or a great master if he chooses to depart from the lay life and become a homeless teacher of true religion. This list was probably written after the stories about Gautama were being told, but it reflects the pattern into which biographies of saviors were supposed to fit.

We may summarize the pattern in this way. A divine figure in a heaven is aware of the problems of humans. The descent is accomplished quickly, but since it is descent into a real human body he must enter materiality as an embryo in the womb of a female human. There is no human male involved in the conception, and the assistance of the angels is not sexual. The baby is born in nearly the normal manner. He is honored by angels and then by humans. Prophets announce that the baby will become a spiritual teacher and make right the miserable current state of human affairs. The story continues with the teaching and mission of the great person, and ends with his ascension to the highest heaven, or his nirvana in the Buddhist case.

How different this pattern is from that of a god disappearing from his heaven and instantly appearing on earth in a spiritual body that appears to be that of a mature human. Rather, the god comes to earth in a real human body, in a body that is born, eats, cries, gets sick, grows wiser, ages, and dies.

When Ganges spirituality (which I discuss in chapter 2)

evolved, the concept of the incarnate savior spread widely within India and beyond. Within India the concept is central to the Krishna tradition, which has had millions of devotees across the centuries, and to Buddhism.[4] Vishnu Hinduism, Buddhism, and Christianity are each based upon the concept of an incarnate master who descended from the heavens, was born to a spiritually pure woman, matured into a spiritual teacher, accomplished his saving mission, and ascended to the heavens.

There are differences among these three traditions' concepts of the incarnation, however. For example, the early Buddhists did not consider the Buddha a god. And Christians believe that the incarnation of Christ was unique, whereas there have been other Buddhas and Vishnu has come down many times.

Although according to each tradition the avatar god is genuinely embodied, the pious followers could hardly resist embellishing the stories with miraculous elements. The conceptions associated with the appearance of a god in a spiritual body came to be applied to the god in a human body as well. This mixing of narrative motifs led to a deification of the *body* of the master, which in turn created inconsistencies in the narrative. Some Buddhists asserted that Gautama could not have perspired or defecated, for was he not the Buddha?[5] Jesus could not have really suffered on the cross or really died, some Christians reasoned, for was he not God himself?

The position that the master's body only *appeared* to be earthly (the docetic heresy) haunted both Buddhism and Christianity in their developing years and eventually led both religions to a compromise position that maintained the humanness of the master's body while also asserting that various miracles surrounded that body's life on earth. But the memory of the master's eating, tiring, and so forth was too strong to permit the total triumph of the docetic, god-in-a-spiritual-body conception. The compromise position that prevailed in both Buddhism and Christianity held that the masters were fully human, yet capable of occasional displays of supernatural bodily powers, such as walking on water or becoming radiant.

Glorifying the account. After a great leader has emerged from among a people and been proved superior in war, statesmanship, arts, or religion, there is an understandable urge on the part of admirers to add further glory to the story by legendizing the leader's infancy and childhood.

One way to glorify the accomplishments of a leader is to exaggerate his humble beginnings. Stories told of Moses and Abe Lincoln use this technique. Another common theme involves the idea that the same personality qualities exemplified by the hero in his mature years were also present in his youth. This motif is used in the stories about the young Krishna and the young Muhammad, for example, as well as the young George Washington.

Other legends of the hero's youth excite the listener with more fantastic claims. A common claim is that the hero or perhaps the hero's parent was a genetic mixture of human and animal. This is a legendary device sometimes used in accounts of the beginning of a new race, as in the story of the "lion race" (the Sinhalese), which peopled the beautiful island of Sri Lanka (Ceylon).[6] Such stories symbolize the way the original leaders of the race bridged the gap that exists between man and beast.

There is an even greater abyss that the young religious leader must span; namely, that between heaven and earth, between the creator and the creatures. The symbolism most useful for this task is a description of the hero as the offspring of that ultimate in mixed marriages—the union of god and human. Conception stories about Gautama and Jesus both tell how the master descends to earth and magically becomes an embryo in the womb of a woman of great moral virtue. This accomplishes the *union of opposites,* which makes possible the mission to provide for humans a means of salvation.

This is the first and perhaps most striking point of comparison between the stories of the births of Jesus and Gautama. In each case the conception occurred without sexual intercourse.

Christians refer to this as the virgin birth. Maya was not a virgin before she conceived Gautama, but in the Buddhist stories she conceives nonsexually, along these lines:[7]

a) Queen Maya took several vows in observance of eight days of special piety in connection with a summer festival. These vows included abstinence from sexual intercourse as well as strict obedience to Buddhist ethical principles such as non-harming.
b) Queen Maya dreamed that a magical white elephant entered through her right side into her womb. This left her with a feeling of great joy.
c) She resolved never to indulge in sexual pleasures again—for they seemed inappropriate now that she had experienced such lasting joy.
d) While the queen carried the embryo she could perceive it through her own flesh. Also, she had no sickness and was unusually healthy and joyous.

The narrative details in the stories of Jesus and Gautama are quite different, but they have in common the idea that their hero descended to earth miraculously, into the womb of a spiritually pure woman, to begin his mission. They also have in common the idea that the woman chosen to be the vehicle of the divine descent should not ever again have sexual intercourse. There is no such stance taken in the New Testament itself; but, as is well known, the tradition developed that Mary was forever virgin—in spite of the references to the brothers of Jesus in the New Testament. For their part, the Buddhist narratives never say explicitly that the reason the mother of a Buddha must die in seven days is that this removes the possibility of future sexual intercourse, but this consideration must surely have been important. Something in the depths of the human consciousness makes sexual intercourse seem incompatible with holiness.

Angels played a role in directing and unfolding the destinies of the two infant saviors. In the Buddhist account there are four divine figures whom I shall call archangels. They carry the queen, asleep on her bed, off to the place of her conception. They watch over her while she is pregnant, and they receive the child when it is born.

An angel plays a large role in the Christian narratives as well, as a bearer of messages from God. Luke identifies the angel as Gabriel. In both the Buddhist and Christian accounts the reader has the impression that there is a plan, a destiny, known to the angels, who are charged with seeing it through to its fulfillment.

The birth. Only Luke's Gospel gives an account of the actual birth of Jesus, so I shall now consider some of the points of comparison between the birth of Jesus according to chapter 2 of Luke and the birth of Gautama according to the Buddhist stories. At first reading, the differences in the stories seem to dominate. In one case we have the birth of a prince to a royal couple of considerable wealth and prestige, whereas Jesus was born to a family of little status or wealth. The young Gautama was honored by the important men of his day, while the young Jesus was born unnoticed by the Hebrew or Roman leaders. Yet there are similarities. Each baby was surrounded by persons and events that, seen in retrospect, mark them destined for greatness. Each was delivered while the mother was on a journey. Neither was born in a house with the assistance of a midwife. Gautama came into the world in the great outdoors—all the major events of his life were to take place in a grove of blossoming trees. Jesus was apparently born in a stable, for Luke says that Mary "laid him in a manger, because there was no place for them in the inn."

The angels rejoice. The next event narrated by Luke was the coming of an angel to shepherds. The angel appeared together with an awesome light and explained to the shepherds the nature of the great event. I quote the relevant verses from Luke alongside a comparable passage from one of the biographies of the Buddha. (Throughout this book I will put the Buddhist texts in the right-hand column.)

And the angels said to them, "Be not afraid; for behold, I bring you good news of a great joy which will come to all the people; for to you is born this day in the city of David a Savior, who is Christ the Lord. And this will be a sign for you: you will find a babe wrapped in swaddling cloths and lying in a manger." And suddenly there was with the angel a multitude of the heavenly host praising God. . . . Luke 2:10-13	On the very day (of his birth) the assembly of the gods in the heaven of the Thirty-three sported rejoicing and shaking their garments, saying, "In the city of Kapilavatthu, to king Suddhodana, a son is born. This boy will sit on the seat of Enlightenment and become a Buddha." Intro. to the Jatakas[8]

In the twentieth century it is difficult to appreciate the role of angels, but formerly they played an important part in the scheme of things. Their main occupation was to sing the praises of the deity. Thus, on the occasion of the birth of Gautama and Jesus the angels sing praises. In both stories they also informed some humans of the great event, announcing the city, the place of the birth, the parents of the baby, and prophesying about the child's glory. What is different in the narratives is the detail surrounding the angels' appearance. In the Buddhist account the angels were seen and heard by an old hermit sage who was able to discern their praising and celebration in heaven because he had unusual psychic powers as a result of years of meditation. He asked the reason for the rejoicing and was given the message quoted above about the birth of a son to King Suddhodana.

Honor to the infant. The Indian sage went at once to pay homage to the infant, as did the shepherds to venerate the infant Jesus. But the encounter of the sage Asita with Gautama is closer to the Simeon story, so I will postpone its conclusion for the time being. For now it is enough to point out that both the Buddhist and Christian narratives want the hearers to know that some persons paid homage to the savior at his descent to and birth into the world of humans.

The Buddhist narrative focuses on the role of the father, once the baby is born, and the mother's role diminishes. (In fact, Maya died seven days after giving birth.) This is very different from the Christian narrative, in which the mother played an important part and the father was completely lost from the account by the time Jesus began his mission. Gautama was raised as a pampered prince, but we can assume that Jesus' childhood in a small Jewish fishing village within an area dominated by Greek-speaking people was quite unlike that of a prince.

Naming the child. The next event reported in Luke's narrative is the ritual of circumcision and naming, which was held on the eighth day after the birth of Jesus, according to Jewish custom. Indians do not practice circumcision, but a naming ceremony was held for Gautama on the fifth day after his birth. He was named Siddhartha, which may be translated as "Success" and which is usually understood as a reference to the fact that he would succeed in his mission. As for the nature of that mission, some accounts say that it was at the naming ceremony that several learned Brahmins did a "reading" of his bodily signs and concluded that he had the thirty-two signs that indicated he would be the greatest person possible. The only question was whether his greatness would manifest itself in the secular realm (a universal monarch) or in the spiritual realm (a fully enlightened Buddha). They were not certain, but one young Brahmin said that, in addition to the thirty-two major signs, he discerned the eighty minor signs that determined that in fact the young boy would eventually become a Buddha. Since the king wanted his son to become a mighty monarch, he undertook to keep from the prince anything that might cause him to choose a spiritual career. The Brahmins advised him that seeing the sufferings of old age, sickness, and death on the one hand and the bliss of a hermit sage on the other would cause him to leave the pleasure-filled life of the palace in search of solutions to life's great problems; so the king ordered that sights such as these should never meet the eyes of his young son. No such attempt to shelter Jesus from the existential contingencies of life was ever made, of course. Gautama grew up in a prosperous, peaceful, and happy kingdom, which he eventually rejected in pursuit of spiritual satisfaction. Jesus grew up in a troubled era, away from the sources of political power or financial security, and very much within the world of the hard-working classes. When Jesus left home to wander and teach, he left behind a very different childhood than did Gautama.

Other versions of the Buddhist narrative put the prophecy that the baby would become a Buddha in the mouth of the sage Asita rather than any of the palace Brahmins. Asita's role has been compared[9] to that of the old sage Simeon, who blessed the baby Jesus in the temple, according to Luke's account:

Now there was a man in Jerusalem, whose name was Simeon, and this man was righteous and devout, looking for the consolation of Israel, and the Holy Spirit was upon him. And it had been revealed to him by the Holy Spirit that he should not see death before he had seen the Lord's Christ. And inspired by the Spirit he came into the temple; and when the parents brought in the child Jesus, to do for him according to the custom of the law, he took him in his arms and blessed God and said, "Lord, now lettest thou thy servant depart in peace, according to thy word; for mine eyes have seen thy salvation which thou has prepared in the presence of all people,	The ascetic had the memory of forty past cycles and of forty to come, eighty in all, and seeing that the Bodhisatta possessed the signs he called to remembrance whether he would become a Buddha or not, and knowing that he would certainly become a Buddha said, "this is a marvellous person," and smiled. Then calling to remembrance whether he should be able to see him when he had become a Buddha, he saw that he would not be able, but having died he could not attain enlightenment through a hundred or even a thousand Buddhas, and would be reborn in the Formless world. And thinking "such a marvellous person, when he has become Buddha, I shall not be able to see: great verily will be my loss," he wept.

a light for revelation to the Gentiles, and for glory to thy people Israel."

And his father and his mother marveled at what was said about him; and Simeon blessed them and said to Mary his mother, "Behold, this child is set for the fall and rising of many in Israel, and for a sign that is spoken against (and a sword will pierce through your own soul also), that thoughts out of many hearts may be revealed."

Luke 2:25-35

The people seeing this asked, "our noble one just now smiled, and then began to weep. Can it be, reverend sir, that there will be any misfortune to our noble son?" "There will be no misfortune to him. Without doubt he will become a Buddha." "Then why didst thou weep?" "Thinking that I shall not be able to see him when he has become Buddha; great verily will be my loss, and lamenting for myself I weep," he said.

Intro. to the Jatakas[10]

In both stories an elderly wise man is the first to inform the parents, or the father at least, that the boy is no ordinary baby. The background assumption is that a sage who has built up spiritual power by his righteous practices has acquired a supernatural discernment that allows him to see and interpret qualities in the young masters that were not apparent to other observers. In both legends the impending death of the sage is referred to, but only in the Buddhist version does the old man lament that he will not be alive when the baby matures.

The wise men honor the child. Matthew's account is quite different from Luke's. Matthew began by stating that Mary conceived Jesus spiritually rather than by sexual intercourse, which agrees with Luke's narrative. But Matthew omitted all detail about the circumstances of the birth, except that it occurred in Bethlehem, and went immediately to the famous story of the visit of the *magi*. *Magi* is from a Persian word that named a class of learned men who sought to master the sciences of their day, including astrology and magic. Elsewhere in early Christianity and in Judaism of that day the term *magi* usually had a bad connotation—what we might call a practitioner of black magic. But in Matthew's account the reference is quite positive. These astrologers from the East, where astrology had been a developed science for centuries, represented the pinnacle of foreign scholarly achievement; and it was they rather than the Hebrews who were able to discern that the baby in the manger in Bethlehem was a very special child. Later the Christian tradition fleshed out Matthew's skeletal story, saying that the wise men were kings, that there were three—or maybe four in an earlier period—and names, ages, and countries were assigned to them.

Similarly the infant Gautama was first adored by the four divine "kings," the archangels who presided over his birth. In addition to this episode, some of the Buddhist biographies relate a later incident in which several sages who had been flying through the air came to earth near the young Gautama to venerate him. Gautama's father was astonished, for normally even a king like himself should pay respect to holy men, but they voluntarily paid homage to his young son. The impression of the Buddhist and Christian stories upon their hearers must have been quite similar: how marvelous that even magical, learned men came from afar to worship the child!

The impact of the star the wise men saw is largely lost upon readers in our time. If we forget for the moment all the paintings we have seen with a dominant star emitting a brilliant light just above Bethlehem, we can read the story in Matthew with a fresh mind and see that it describes some astrologers who were searching the sky for a new star that would announce the birth of a master.

This same astrological perspective is apparent in the Buddhist accounts when they say that the infant Gautama was born on the day of the full moon and when a certain constellation was in a certain position. It is also said that at the time of Gautama's birth a marvelous, supernatural light spread throughout the universe and was seen by the various supernatural creatures, who then praised the great event.[11]

The Indian wise men mentioned above did not give gifts to the infant Gautama as Matthew's wise men did to Jesus; but in some versions of the story of the sage Asita previously discussed, the king gives gifts to Asita, according to etiquette, and Asita immediately gives them to the infant. The world's most valued items were given to symbolize the even greater value of the infant. Jesus received "gold and frankincense and myrrh"—prime items on the East-West trade route; while the infant Gautama was similarly given "costly jewels and precious substances."[12]

This comparison of the descent and birth of the two masters has focused on the points of convergence in the two narratives; so before discussing the similarities in their later lives, I wish to call attention to some of the differences in the stories.

As an example of a Buddhist episode that has no biblical counterpart, I would note that the Buddhist biographies typically state that at the birth of Gautama there occurred several cosmic events such as earthquakes and supernatural lights. One of the most fanciful of the accounts, the Lalita-vistara, relates that the sun, moon, rivers, workmen, everything came to a standstill. The idea that the key events in the life of a master are of such import that the whole cosmos responds is not missing in the New Testament, as the reference to the "star in the East" shows; but in the biblical account it is at the death of Jesus that such events as earthquakes are said to have happened.

Another detail that is told of Gautama but not of Jesus is that the infant Gautama, as soon as he had been received from Maya and placed on the ground, took seven steps to the north and proclaimed loudly that he was king of the world and declared, "This is my last birth." The Christian texts refrain from attributing to the newborn Jesus any abilities as precocious as walking and speaking.

The Buddhist narratives also relate that seven other significant creatures were born or came into being at the same time as Gautama. These seven were to play important parts in the later life of the Buddha. They are his future wife, his charioteer, and a peer at court, his elephant and horse, the tree under which he was to be enlightened, and four treasure-filled vases. The biblical account does not indulge in this theme, except that Luke connects the birth of John with that of Jesus, though he does not have them born on the same day. The effect of this theme in both Luke and the Buddhist narratives is to enhance the sense of historical importance surrounding the birth of the master in the world.

The physical signs discernible on Gautama's body play an important role in the Buddhist narrative and in later Buddhist art, after the prohibition against imaging the Buddha was broken. Early Christian tradition is incredibly silent concerning the physical appearance of its master. The very early Buddhist accounts were also, some scholars believe, but the later biographies and works of art are quite another matter.

Matthew's account, it should be noted, contains some incidents which have no Buddhist equivalents—nor are there parallels in the other three Gospels. According to Matthew's account Jesus is taken to Egypt for a few years to escape the vengeful wrath of the tyrannical ruler Herod.[13] The Buddhist narrative could have no such episode, for Gautama's own father was the ruler.

How Masters Live

Both the Buddhist and Christian narratives contain only one episode about the master between his infancy and his spiritual awakening, but in each case that episode sets the stage for the master's career.

The fuller Buddhist accounts of this instance vary greatly, but all of them seem to derive from a brief autobiographic statement contained in one of Gautama's sermons.[14] At a time in his quest for enlightenment when he was discouraged and about to abandon food deprivation as a spiritual technique, he recalls a profitable childhood experience:

> I thought of a time when my Sakyan father was working[15] and I was sitting in the cool shade of a rose-apple tree: quite secluded from sensual desires, secluded from unprofitable things I had entered

upon and abode in the first meditation, which is accompanied by thinking and exploring with happiness and pleasure born of seclusion. I thought: Might that be the way to enlightenment? Then following up that memory there came the recognition that this was the way to enlightenment.[16]

This childhood recollection set Gautama onto a middle path between torturing and indulging his body. Put more positively, he abandoned severe asceticism as a spiritual technique and took up the practice of sitting comfortably in a secluded spot where he meditated upon existential problems such as suffering.

The only known event in Jesus' childhood is, of course, his prolonged discussion with the scholars at the Jerusalem temple. To fully appreciate this story we have to realize what a contrast there was, for better or worse, between a village house of prayer (synagogue) and the large, stone temple complex at Jerusalem, with its throne seat for God in the inner sanctum, its altar for animal sacrifices in the courtyard, and its numerous resident priests and scholars. Here, according to the story, Jesus adumbrates his later teaching career by besting or at least amazing the Hebrew scholars at their own game, the application of scripture to life. The Buddhist and Christian stories are really quite different, but both express the idea that the masters were serious in their spiritual pursuits even as youths.

In spite of the early prophecies of greatness, their being venerated as infants, and their brief, youthful forays into spiritual matters, Gautama and Jesus did not begin their spiritual quests in earnest until approximately age thirty. As with the stories of their infancies, there are several episodes in the stories of their early careers that are similar enough to make comparisons fruitful.

Gautama began his spiritual quest when the protective shield his father placed around him broke down. According to most of the accounts, his naïveté about the problems of life was overcome by the famous "four sights" he had while riding in his chariot through a park near the palace. Despite his father's precautions against just this sort of occurrence, Gautama happened to see a sick man, a decrepit old man, and a dead man. These made him aware of the problems of life, which became the enemy he sought to overcome. The fourth and final sight, of a calm hermitic monk, suggested a solution to Gautama. He vowed to depart "from the world," to leave the world of houses, happiness, and security. Instead he would abide out of doors and spend his time pursuing spiritual practices in an effort to break the wheel of birth, suffering, and death that plagues all persons, according to his view of human reincarnation.

Gautama began the way all serious students of higher knowledge began in the sixth century B.C. in India. He left home and family, put on a ragged garment or a yellow one—the uniform of the holy man—and journeyed toward the Ganges River area. There in various localities along the Ganges were gathered the spiritual masters of the day. Gautama apprenticed himself to various of these traveling professors before deciding to practice severe asceticism on his own. For six years he practiced food and fluid deprivation, exposure to the burning sun or bone-chilling rain, and other means of torturing the body for the sake of the spirit. Then he gave up severe asceticism, took food in moderation, and began to practice a wakeful contemplation, which culminated in spiritual enlightenment while he was sitting under a tree in a solitary place.

Most of these events in Gautama's life have no parallel in the story of Jesus. Luke's account of Jesus' life continues with the story of his baptism by John in the Jordan River, at which time the Holy Spirit is said to have descended upon him and a voice from heaven was heard saying that Jesus was God's son. The next episode in his life was his period of fasting and spiritual searching in solitude.

Quest and temptation. According to Mark's version, probably the oldest account we have, the Spirit took Jesus into the desert immediately after his baptism by John in the Jordan.

Two Masters

The stay in the desert lasted forty days, we are told, and during that time Satan tempted him and the presence of wild animals threatened, but the angels helped Jesus. Luke's and Matthew's accounts are more detailed and add two factors that are relevant to my comparison with the temptation of Gautama. Luke and Matthew both add to Mark's story the report that Jesus fasted during his time in the wilderness. This compares with the period of severe fasting and other austerities practiced by Gautama for six years. In Luke's and Matthew's accounts we learn the nature of Satan's temptation. We note that Gautama also had a conversation with the Tempter while he was fasting. To facilitate a comparison I will cite the two stories. (Namucī is another name for Māra, "Death," the Buddhist Satan. He is also nicknamed "The Black One" in this passage.)

And Jesus, full of the Holy Spirit, returned from the Jordan, and was led by the Spirit for forty days in the wilderness, tempted by the devil. And he ate nothing in those days; and when they were ended, he was hungry.

The devil said to him, "If you are the Son of God, command this stone to become bread."

And Jesus answered him, "It is written, 'Man shall not live by bread alone.' "

And the devil took him up, and showed him all the kingdoms of the world in a moment of time, and said to him, "To you I will give all this authority and their glory; for it has been delivered to me, and I give it to whom I will. If you, then, will worship me, it shall all be yours."

And Jesus answered him, "It is

As I strove to subdue myself
Beside the broad Nerañjarā [River]
Absorbed unflinchingly to gain
The true surcease of bondage here,
Namucī came and spoke to me
With words all garbed in pity thus:
"O you are thin and you are pale,
And you are in death's presence too;
A thousand parts are pledged to death,
But life still holds one part of you.
Live, sir! Life is the better way;
You can gain merit if you live;
Come, live the Holy Life and pour
Libations on the holy fires,
And thus a world of merit gain.
What can you do

written, 'You shall worship the 'Lord your God, and him only shall you serve.' "

And he took him to Jerusalem, and set him on the pinnacle of the temple, and said to him, "If you are the Son of God, throw yourself down from here; for it is written, 'He will give his angels charge of you, to guard you,' and 'On their hands they will bear you up, lest you strike your foot against a stone.' "

And Jesus answered him, "It is said, 'You shall not tempt the Lord your God.' "

And when the devil had ended every temptation, he departed from him until an opportune time.

Luke 4:1-13

by struggling now?"

[Gautama replied]
"Your first squadron is Sense-Desires,
Your second is called Boredom, then
Hunger and Thirst compose the third,
And Craving is the fourth in rank,
The fifth is Sloth and Accidy,
While Cowardice lines up as sixth,
Uncertainty is seventh, the eighth
Is Malice paired with Obstinacy;
Gain, Honour and Renown, besides
An ill-won Notoriety,
Self-praise and Denigrating Others—
These are your squadrons, Namucī;
These are the Black One's fighting squadrons;
None but the brave will conquer them."

Sutta-nipāta 3.2[17]

The settings of these two accounts are almost identical. Both masters, while in their early thirties, entered into a prolonged retreat in an isolated area near a river. While in retreat they undertook a severe fast and came face to face with the devil himself. It is accepted today that people may suffer horrible visions as a result of food deprivation, so we might interpret these stories as accounts of what happened within the minds of the two struggling masters. In fact many Buddhists, and at least some Christians, do interpret this episode psychologically. On the other hand, the stories themselves give no indication that they are narrating visions; rather they describe a realistic dialogue between the master and the Lord of Death.

In each account the master was enticed to use his supernatural power for worldly purposes. Both refused, for they were intent upon directing their spiritual power toward a higher cause. What made the temptation so timely was that both were weak from hunger, and in both the Buddhist and Christian traditions there is the idea that the devil knows the best times to tempt humans. (Anyone who has shopped for groceries just before dinner can verify this.)

The actual words used by Satan differ considerably from those of Mara, however. Satan tempted Jesus to break his fast, to rule the world, and to put God's protection to the test. Jesus of course refused, and argued against the devil's entreaties by quoting from the Hebrew scriptures. Jesus quoted from the book of Deuteronomy, while the devil attempted to play the same game by quoting from one of the psalms.

Mara's main line of temptation was to point out to Gautama that the life of a hermit ascetic, like that of Alice's palace guard, was terrible hard. What's more, Mara argued, there was no real need for such a difficult life-style, for one can be admirably religious while at the same time being the lord of an estate or a king. Mara's point was the one that is always argued by persons critical of monasticism, whether hermitic or cloistered; namely, that a person can do more good by living in the world righteously than by withdrawing from society. By saying "you can gain merit" Mara advanced what must have been the prevailing religious opinion of the day—that doing good deeds generated spiritual power (merit), which brought one happiness in this life and in the next. Gautama's rejection of Mara employed an elaborate metaphor that compared Mara to a general whose army consists of such things as hunger, thirst, cowardice, and the desire for fame and glory. Gautama renewed his resolve to resist just such impulses so Mara would not be able to tempt him from his mission.

There are several encounters between Gautama and Mara narrated in each of the Buddhist biographies and sermons, and the biographies tell the stories variously. Some of these put words in the mouth of Mara that are closer to the biblical stories than the account I just cited. For example, the Mahāvastu[18] and several other accounts say that the devil tempted Gautama to become a *ruler over the whole world.* This made sense in the Buddhist context because Gautama was an heir apparent and the prophets at his birth had forecast that he would rule a mighty kingdom extending to the ends of the earth in all four directions.[19]

In another account the three daughters of Mara, who were sensuality personified according to some Buddhist commentators, offered Gautama the rule of the whole world if he would leave his tree of enlightenment and make love to them:

> We promise you shall reign, as Sakra [God] does in heaven,
> On every hand surrounded by lovely damsels;
> Yea! like the gods in all the heavens,
> Unequalled, with no competitor or any rival,
> If only you will not refuse our love.[20]

The narrative continues in a way that reminds us of Jesus' stay in the desert or wilderness near the Jordan, where wild beasts and danger abounded:

> Oh! Sakyaputra [i.e., Gautama], thou art yet young and of vigorous body—go, enjoy the sweets of your palace. There are but few people in this wild desert; the beasts prowl about for their prey. I fear much for your safety; arise then, Oh son of Sakya! return to thy palace, leave this place—search no longer after that wisdom which is so hard to find; but indulge in the pleasures of life, and forget thy present quest.[21]

Gautama resisted this temptation to rule and indulge himself with the observation that all sensual pleasures are temporary. Their lifespan is limited, like ripe fruit hanging on a tree, like a dream or a bolt of lightning.

Mara continued the temptation by pointing out to Gautama

that the world greatly needed a righteous ruler, but Gautama again resisted on the grounds that his goal was to achieve the ultimate spiritually, not politically.

In one of the earliest of the Buddhist biographical passages[22] Mara tempted Gautama to transmute a mountain into gold. Edmunds has compared this with Satan's tempting Jesus to turn a rock into bread.

The Buddhist accounts are themselves so diverse that it is difficult to say just what occurred between Gautama and Mara, and on which occasions. Nevertheless it is possible to make some general comparisons about the temptations of Jesus and Gautama. As mentioned already, the settings of the temptations are almost identical, if we follow those Buddhist accounts which place a temptation within Gautama's period of fasting and searching.

The tempters are also quite similar.[23] The assumption behind both the Christian and Buddhist accounts is that the devil is in some realistic but limited way the ruler of a domain that includes the earth and its inhabitants. It is further taken for granted that this ruler is the lord of death who does not want any human to escape his sphere of power. To prevent such a thing from happening he leads astray any human who is making serious progress toward an escape from his rule. His favorite means is to play upon a person's desire for comfort and security. Yet Jesus and Gautama were able to resist the devil's temptations and emerged from the struggle more determined than ever. The positive ending to the story suggests that in the long run the devil's role may not be as negative and destructive as it might seem.

To continue the comparison it should be noted that Gautama and Jesus responded to the devil in different ways, according to their different backgrounds. Gautama, who did not believe in a fatherly god who takes personal interest in the salvation quests of humans, did not resist the devil's temptations in the name of a god. Rather he resisted on the grounds of destiny and merit; that is, on the grounds that it was he himself who had perfected his generosity, tenacity, and wisdom through hundreds of years of striving over the course of many lives. The more theological response of Jesus is to appeal to the understanding of God as embodied in the Hebrew scriptures, a fatherly God who takes an interest in the spiritual quest of humans.

The conclusions of the stories are similar. Both young masters leave their seclusion and take up a traveling life of teaching, while the devil vows to follow them in anticipation of a moment of weakness.[24]

At this point in the chronology of the two masters an event of paramount importance in the life of Gautama occurred. Having left the security of life in a home, having practiced self-torture for six years without achieving a spiritual breakthrough, and having taken up the practice of meditative reflection on the problems of embodiment, Gautama achieved the long-awaited climax of his many lives of spiritual questing while meditating through the night under a tree in a pleasant spot near a river. That night his arduous efforts at mental perfection were rewarded by a breakthrough into the realm of total understanding and nirvanic bliss. This event became the most important one in his life, in the eyes of later Buddhists, and it has no close parallel in the story of Jesus. The Gospel writers do not mention exactly when Jesus felt that he was ready to begin his teaching and healing career. They make it clear that this decision was reached sometime during the period of his baptism and his stay in the wilderness. There is also the suggestion that the arrest of John the Baptist played a role in Jesus' decision.

Jesus first found an audience for his teaching in the sabbath meetings at the village synagogues. Gautama's first audience consisted of five ascetics who had previously accompanied him during his period of fasting. Both Gautama and Jesus took up the life-style of a traveling spiritual master, for which there was a long tradition in India. The established pattern was that a spiritual teacher would travel from village to village teaching, answering questions, and giving advice to the people. The wandering holy man had the fewest possible possessions and depended entirely upon voluntary contributions of the villagers for his sustenance. These contributions usually consisted of modest amounts of food daily, and gifts of clothing and medicines as needed. Some of these wandering holy men were accompanied by disciples who looked to the master for leadership in both wisdom and discipline. No one knows when this tradition first began in India, but it was well established in the sixth century B.C. when Gautama followed it, and it continues today.[25]

The biblical accounts of the life of Jesus imply that Jesus followed a life-style very much like that of the Indian holy man. He traveled from village to village, lived off the hospitality of members of the villages, gave teaching and advice when requested, gathered around himself a group of disciples, and lived very modestly. Some of these points deserve additional comment. For example, both Jesus and Gautama seem to have made it a practice to accept hospitality from the first person who offered it in a particular village, without regard for the social status of the host or hostess. This deliberate blindness to social status more than once got both masters into trouble with the ruling aristocracies. Gautama angered the nobility of a city when he accepted an invitation to eat at the house of the city's courtesan. The status-conscious noblemen were offended that Gautama chose to dine with a prostitute rather than with them. Sometimes Gautama did accept food from important persons, so it would seem his approach was to not discriminate according to wealth or status. Similarly Jesus was condemned for eating in the homes of sinners and prostitutes, and some of his parables make the point that rich leaders of the Jewish people will by no means be first to dine at the eschatological banquet table.

The masters' willingness to associate with and accept food from lower-class and despised people also forms the background to the following stories about accepting water from a forbidden woman. To appreciate such stories as these it is necessary to realize what important social acts the acceptance of food and drink were traditionally. Even in contemporary secularized societies without official class distinctions, to eat or drink with people is to accept them. The psychological power of eating and drinking together is by no means lost today, it is merely lessened. Indeed, this was dramatized in recent times when American blacks demanded the right to be served in the same restaurants with whites, repudiating the idea that separate facilities could be equal. In many cultures, especially that of ancient India, it was also thought to imply equality if one received food or drink from someone, so the rules of class forbade accepting such things from someone of lower class. Here are the stories, one about Jesus and the other about the monk Ananda, who was the personal attendant to Gautama during Gautama's old age:

There came a woman of Samaria to draw water. Jesus said to her, "Give me a drink."

The Samaritan woman said to him, "How is it that you, a Jew, ask a drink of me, a woman of Samaria?" For Jews have no dealings with Samaritans.

Jesus answered her, "If you knew the gift of God, and who it is that is saying to you, 'Give me a drink,' you would have asked him, and he would have given you living water. . . . Everyone who drinks of this water will thirst again, but whoever drinks of the water that I shall give him will never thirst; the water that I shall give him will become in him a spring of water welling up to eternal life."

After his round, and having finished his meal he approached a certain well. At that time a Mātanga [outcast] girl was at the well drawing water. So the elder Ananda said to the Mātanga girl, "give me water, sister, I wish to drink." At this she replied, "I am a Mātanga girl, reverend Ananda." "I do not ask you, sister, about your family or caste, but if you have any water left over, give it me, I wish to drink." Then she gave Ananda the water. Ananda having drunk it went away, and she finding in Ananda's body, mouth, and voice a good and excellent sign fell into meditation, and awaking passion thought, may the noble Ananda be my husband. My mother is a

The woman said to him, "Sir, give me this water, that I may not thirst, nor come here to draw."
John 4:7, 9-10, 13-15

great magician, she will be able to bring him.
Divyāvadāna[26]

The similarity lies in the acceptance the masters and their followers give all humans regardless of social status or nationality. Gautama and Jesus both enjoyed considerable honor and popularity in some periods of their careers as wandering masters. However, neither of them was well received in his hometown. Jesus was nearly killed (Luke 4:29), and Gautama's fellow townsmen refused to pay him any special honor, although they did not wish him any harm. Tension mounted for Gautama when some of the youth of the town wished to become monks, so Gautama made a rule that no child could be accepted into the order without his parents' permission.[27] In spite of these problems, eventually Gautama's son and stepmother became members of his order, and Jesus' brothers later became leaders of the early church.

Gautama and Jesus also met with opposition concerning their attitudes toward liturgy, for both were less concerned about the formalities of ritual than were the religious leaders of their day. Gautama was quite ready to reform all those existing Brahmanical rituals which involved harming animals or humans—it seems that some of the feudal lords drove their slaves mercilessly in making elaborate preparations for some of the more extensive sacrifices. In place of the harming rituals Gautama substituted new rituals that did no injury to human or animal and that had as their goal the establishment of a peaceful, harmonious society that paid respect to anyone who had become spiritually developed. Jesus resisted the legalistic interpretations of Hebrew traditions, seemingly ignored the role of temple sacrifices, and eventually became the center of a new set of rituals for his followers. Yet neither Jesus nor Gautama seems to have made cultic reform the principal goal; rather their reforms grew out of their life-styles and teachings.

The notion of spiritual purity and defilement underlay the ritual observances of the Brahmanic Hinduism of Gautama's day and the Judaism of Jesus' era. Each master resisted the prohibitions that had been designed to avoid spiritual pollution. Jesus insisted that "the sabbath was made for man"; Gautama said, "Ask not about one's birth, ask about his character."

Speaking against food taboos, which were motivated by the fear of spiritual pollution, Jesus and Gautama insisted that it is not what one eats but what one thinks and does that makes one morally impure:

Do you not see that whatever goes into the mouth passes into the stomach, and so passes on? But what comes out of the mouth proceeds from the heart, and this defiles a man. For out of the heart come evil thoughts, murder, adultery, fornication, theft, false witness, slander. These are what defile a man; but to eat with unwashed hands does not defile a man. Matt. 15:17-20	One does not become pure by washing . . . ; he who casts away every sin both great and small, he, because he casts away sins, is a holy man. Udanavarga 33.13[28] Destroying life, killing, cutting, binding, stealing, speaking lies, fraud and deceptions, worthless reading, intercourse with another's wife,—this is defilement, but not the eating of flesh. Sutta-nipāta no. 242[29]

The point here is that both the Buddhist and Christian masters shifted the responsibility for purity inward, to the heart of the individual. Jesus seems to have decided that the washing of hands before eating was a dispensable ritual, and Gautama ruled that it was not the actual eating of meat that defiled one, but rather the act of killing the animal in the first place.

Another similarity concerns the way both Jesus and Gautama dealt with their disciples. The accounts of Jesus' calling his disciples do not have a parallel in Buddhism, but the instructions he gave to his disciples do. For example, Jesus spent a great deal of his time healing the sick, and he indicated that his disciples should do likewise. A dramatic statement of this expectation occurs in the story of the final judgment contained in the twenty-fifth chapter of Matthew's Gospel. There Jesus told of the persons who will to their surprise receive the praise of the Son of man when he arrives in judgment. I cite part of this story alongside a similar point that Gautama made after he had himself tended the putrid sores of a leper:

And the King will answer them, "Truly, I say to you, as you did it to one of the least of these my brethren, you did it to me." Matt. 25:40	Whosoever, O monks, would wait upon me, let him wait on the sick. Mahāvagga 8.26[30]

Jesus and Gautama made demands upon their disciples that were too much for some would-be followers. Jesus sternly warned that once one had put his hand to the plow there should be no looking back, and Gautama preached a whole sermon on the pitfalls that threaten the career of the celibate disciple. Neither master attempted to make the spiritual path sound simple or easy, and both experienced setbacks when followers returned to their former life-styles, but a core of dedicated ones remained with each of them.[31]

The most serious obstacle for the disciples of Jesus and Gautama was homelessness, the total lack of security concerning even basic needs such as food, clothing, and shelter. Yet both masters considered the homeless life-style to be necessary:

And a scribe came up and said to him, "Teacher, I will follow you wherever you go." And Jesus said to him, "Foxes have holes, and birds of the air have nests; but the Son of man has nowhere	The thoughtful exert themselves; they do not delight in an abode; like swans who have left their lake they leave their house and home.

to lay his head." Another of the disciples said to him, "Lord, let me first go and bury my father." But Jesus said to him, "Follow me, and leave the dead to bury their own dead."

Matt. 8:19-22

Those who have no accumulation [of property] who eat according to knowledge, who have perceived [the nature of] release and unconditioned freedom, their path is difficult to understand like that [the flight] of birds through the sky.

PDh (R) 91-92

Both of these sayings imply that the true followers must abandon all thoughts of security and sensual pleasures.

Jesus and Gautama organized their disciples and sent them out as missionaries, bringing the words and work of the master to a larger audience. According to Mark, Jesus sent out the twelve disciples with special instructions, for the purposes of preaching repentance, exorcising evil spirits, and applying medicines to the sick. Matthew and Luke have similar accounts of the sending of the twelve, but Luke also narrates that Jesus later commissioned seventy disciples. I will cite this latter account together with a Buddhist account of Gautama's missionary charge to sixty of his disciples:

After this the Lord appointed seventy others, and sent them on ahead of him, two by two, into every town and place where he himself was about to come. And he said to them, "The harvest is plentiful, but the laborers are few. . . . Carry no purse, no bag, no sandals; and salute no one on the road. Whatever house you enter, first say, 'Peace be to this house!' . . . And remain in the same house, eating and drinking what they provide, for the laborer deserves his wages; do not

And then there were sixty-one Arahants in the world. Then the Blessed One addressed the Bhikkhus: "Bhikkhus, . . . You are free from all shackles whether human or divine. Go now and wander for the welfare and happiness of many, out of compassion for the world, for the benefit, welfare and happiness of gods and men. Teach the Law that is good in the beginning, good in the middle and good in the end, with the meaning and the letter. Explain a Holy Life that is utterly

go from house to house. Whenever you enter a town and they receive you, eat what is set before you; heal the sick in it and say to them, 'The kingdom of God has come near to you.' But whenever you enter a town and they do not receive you, say, 'Even the dust of your town that clings to our feet, we wipe off against you; nevertheless know this, that the kingdom of God has come near.'"
Luke 10:1-11

perfect and pure. There are creatures with little dust on their eyes who will be lost through not hearing the Law. Some will understand the Law. I shall go to Uruvelā, to Senānigāma, to teach the Law."
Book of Discipline[32]

Jesus' prohibition against carrying purses, though not found in the Buddhist text cited above, is in accordance with early Buddhist regulations that prohibited the monks from carrying or dealing with money (gold, etc.). I am not aware of Buddhists' being forbidden to carry a bag, but they were told not to wear sandals while going for alms. To "salute no one on the road" is not a Buddhist injunction, but the monks were told to remain silent while going for alms. The injunction "do not go from house to house" is the opposite of the Buddhist practice, which is to go from house to house, receiving a small amount of food from each willing household. Gautama, unlike Jesus, did not instruct his disciples to curse the town that refused them.

The reader should not make too much of the difference in going forth to preach "repentance" as opposed to "the Law." The word translated here as "Law" is in Sanskrit *dharma,* which embraces several English concepts such as righteousness, true doctrine, reality, and religion. The main difference between the message of these earliest Buddhist and Christian missionaries is not between law and gospel but between "change your hearts" and "change your hearts before God."

How Masters Return

Having descended from heaven and accomplished his mission, the divine master next turned his attention to preparing for his return. The most important part of the preparation was that of gathering and training a group of disciples who could continue the work in the master's absence. Jesus' followers became the "church," which is considered the body of Christ; and Gautama's became the "sangha," revered as the third of the three precious jewels (the other two are the Buddha and the Dharma). Here is the way the masters themselves expressed this important concern.

And this gospel of the kingdom will be preached throughout the whole world, as a testimony to all nations; and then the end will come. Matt. 24:14	I shall not pass into Nirvāna till this religion of mine is successful, prosperous, widespread, popular, ubiquitous; in a word, made thoroughly public among men. Mahāparinibbāna Sutta[33]

Transfiguration. One way in which Jesus and Gautama prepared their disciples for the death of the master was to allow a small group of the disciples to witness a transfiguration. (Tathāgato is another title for the Buddha.)

And after six days Jesus took with him Peter and James and John his brother, and led them up a high mountain apart. And he was transfigured before them, and his face shone like the sun, and his garments became white as light. And behold, there appeared to them Moses and Elijah, talking ith him.

And Peter said to Jesus, "Lord, it is well that we are here; if you wish, I will make three booths here, one for you and one for Moses and one for Elijah."

He was still speaking, when lo, a bright cloud overshadowed

St. Anando placed upon the person of the Lord that pair of gold-cloth robes. . . . And when so placed upon the person of the Lord, it appeared bereft of its brightness.

And St. Anando said unto the Lord: "Wonderful, O Lord! Marvelous, O Lord! that the color of the Tathāgato's skin should be so pure and purified."

"There are two occasions, Anando, when the color of a Tathāgato's skin becomes pure and exceeding purified. What are the two?

"On the night, Anando,

them, and a voice from the cloud said, "This is my beloved Son, with whom I am well pleased; listen to him."

When the disciples heard this, they fell on their faces, and were filled with awe.

But Jesus came and touched them, saying "Rise, and have no fear."

And when they lifted up their eyes, they saw no one but Jesus only.

Matt. 17:1-8

wherein a Tathāgato is supernally enlightened with incomparable and perfect enlightenment, and on the night when he enters Nirvāna with that kind of Nirvāna which leaves no substrata behind.... And now, Anando, this day, in the third watch of the night, in the garden ground of Kusinārā, in the sāl-grove of the Mallians, between the twin sāl-trees, will take place the Tathāgato's passage into Nirvāna.

Dīgha-nikāya no. 16[34]

The circumstances surrounding these two transfigurations are quite different, as are the disciples' reactions, but there is the basic similarity that both Jesus' and Gautama's bodies became radiant in a supernatural way.

The Christian Gospels and also the Buddhist account connect the transfiguration of the master with his prediction of his own death. Jesus told his disciples that in fact Elijah had already come and that he, Jesus, would soon be killed. Gautama explained that such a glowing of the skin happens twice in the life of a master: at the time of his enlightenment and before his death. Jesus' transfiguration occurred before his death, but was there also a transfiguration at the time of Jesus' enlightenment? Not unless we consider the descent of the spirit upon Jesus at the time of his baptism as functionally similar. The descent of the spirit upon Jesus, the emission of light from Gautama, and the glowing of their persons serve to mark the masters as men of extraordinary spiritual power.

Forgiving evildoers. Throughout their careers the two masters converted people from a life of evil to a life of good. Having themselves overcome the self-centeredness of ordinary mortals, they were able to forgive others with seeming effortlessness. Gautama's approach was to teach right understanding so that a follower's personality could be transformed, after which the person would do meritorious rather than evil deeds and thus avoid future punishment. Jesus put even more emphasis on forgiveness, because for him it was necessary for a person to be "right" before a personal God.

Forgiveness plays a role in the stories of the deaths of both Gautama and Jesus. Gautama died from an illness caused by a food offering, yet he instructed his disciples in no way to blame the impoverished man who had made the offering. Jesus also forgave and converted one of the two thieves who were crucified with him, according to the account in Luke's gospel. Edmunds has compared this conversion of the condemned thief with the story of Gautama's conversion of a murderous highwayman who was named Finger-garland because he wore a necklace strung with the fingers of his victims. Finger-garland attempted to rob and kill Gautama, but by a miracle Gautama remained just out of his reach. Finally the killer gave up, took moral instruction from the master, and entered the order of disciples. The villagers had difficulty accepting the new monk, but Gautama assured them that he was a transformed person and that they should now revere him as a person who had controlled his passions. The two stories have vastly different settings and develop along different lines, but they both illustrate the power of the master to transform even the worst humans.

Conquering death. Ordinary persons are conquered by death, but masters conquer death. In another book I have interpreted Gautama's last words to his disciples as meaning "Death conquers all, so conquer death."[35] Both masters did die, of course, so the meaning of conquering death must lie elsewhere than in the realm of physical immortality. Put mythically, the masters' conquest of death means that they transcended the domain and power of the devil, the Lord of Death. Neither master proved vulnerable to the control of the devil. This is expressed in the Buddhist biographies[36] by an episode in which the devil tempted Gautama to die early in life,

Two Masters

to enjoy the bliss of nirvana right away rather than bothering to become a traveling teacher. Gautama rejected this counsel, of course, just as Jesus in very different circumstances refused to abandon his mission in order to avoid persecution and death (see John 10:17-18).

Put in other terms, Gautama's conquest of death meant that unlike other persons he would never again be reborn in any body whatsoever. And Jesus' conquest of death was manifest in his appearances to his disciples after his crucifixion and in the belief that he arose and ascended into the heavens to be again with God.

A grandiose way of expressing the claim that the master is in charge of his fate in a way that ordinary persons are not is to claim that if he wished to do so, the master could stay alive for the entire length of a world epoch:

The crowd answered him, "We have heard from the law that the Christ remains for ever. How can you say that the Son of man must be lifted up?" John 12:34	Now, Anando, the Tathāgato has practist [sic] perfected these [spiritual qualities]; and if he so should wish, the Tathāgato could remain [on earth] for the aeon. Mahāparinibbāna Sutta[37]

The Greek text of John reads more literally "that the Christ remains into the aeon," which is an idiomatic expression meaning "till the end of this era," or simply "forever." Scholars cannot say exactly what Hebrew text the crowd has in mind here, when it is said that according to scripture the Messiah is to live "forever."[38] Perhaps this was a popular conception that was commonly believed to be scriptural. At any rate, Jesus skirted the claim and repeated that he would be with them only a little longer. Gautama expressed the same belief as the crowd in the Christian account, but went on to tell Ananda that in fact he would die.

The earthquakes. The deaths of both masters were cosmic events, as the earthquakes in the stories show:

And behold, the curtain of the temple was torn in two, from top to bottom; and the earth shook, and the rocks were split; the tombs also were opened, and many bodies of the saints who had fallen asleep were raised. Matt. 27:51-52	When the Lord entered into Nirvāna, a great earthquake, terrific and tremendous, accompanied his entry into Nirvāna; and the drums of the angels rolled. Mahāparinibbāna Sutta[39]

It is common in Buddhist accounts for there to be earthquakes punctuating the dramatic, climactic moments in the life of the master. Only Matthew's account of the death of Jesus includes this motif. Matthew relates that an earthquake with thunder occurred at the death of Jesus, just as the "drums of the angels" sounded at Gautama's death.

Ascension. Essential to the completion of the story of an avatar, a god-come-down, is the account of the ascension of the god. The story of the ascension of Jesus is well known, but it should be noted that the account of Gautama's entering into nirvāna is an ascension story also. The narratives are by no means identical, however. Jesus was first miraculously restored to life, and according to the accounts of the empty tomb and the touching of his hand wounds, we are to take this as a restoration of the physical body. Then after staying a while on earth Jesus ascended through the clouds into the heavens, to be at the right hand of God, it is said.

There is no physical resurrection or ascension in the story of Gautama. On the contrary, Gautama had striven to find *release from embodiment.* In the context of Buddhist thought it would be absurd to think of an embodied ascension. Persons who "go to heaven," in Buddhist thought, receive bodies appropriate to their ethereal existence, but the state of eternal bliss, nirvana, is beyond all physical dimension and description, beyond heaven and earth. Buddhism remains imprecise, perhaps necessarily so, as to what "thing" (a soul?) enters nirvana, but the symbolism is that of ascension, as the concluding portion of the account reveals. Gautama meditated up and down through

Two Masters

the levels of transcendental consciousness, and then up to the fourth level from which he passed into nirvana. His disciples cremated his corpse and distributed the ashes as relics over which burial mounds (stupas or pagodas) were built as memorials and places of veneration.

Veneration of the returned master. As the practice of venerating Gautama at the memorial stupas became more and more popular with the passing centuries, Buddhist thought put more emphasis on the divinity of the master. This emphasis resulted in the nearly complete deification of the Buddha in the *Mahayana* (Mahāyāna) school of Buddhism, and it had a considerable impact on the earlier, more conservative Buddhist sects as well. To justify such worship, the later Buddhists told stories about how Gautama had accepted the veneration of humans while he was alive, which set the precedent for later veneration. It was remembered or imagined that as a prince and later as a Buddha, Gautama was glorified by hundreds of persons. These people bowed low before him, circled him respectfully—clockwise, so that their right hands would be always toward the holy man. When he traveled, the people made the road more passable, sometimes paving it with leaves and flowers. And if humans did not do this, nature herself provided blossoming trees, even out of season.

Christians also worshiped the master and came to look upon him as a manifestation of the deity. They, too, looked to the stories of the master for precedent-setting accounts of veneration. The story of the visit of the magi served this purpose well, as did the accounts of royal treatment given Jesus as he rode into Jerusalem on a road paved with palm leaves shortly before his death.

There were many other examples of veneration available in the biographies. Both masters, for example, had been revered by a woman:

And standing behind him at his feet, weeping, she began to wet	She came swiftly, clasped his ankles, placed his feet round her

his feet with her tears, and wiped them with the hair of her head, and kissed his feet, and anointed them with the ointment.
Luke 7:38

head, and did reverence to him according to her desire.[40]

The woman who venerated Gautama's feet was his wife, who had remained devoted to him during their long separation, since his departure from home. In contrast, the woman who anointed the feet of Jesus is said to have been a sinner, so the companions of Jesus were upset by the incident. A different Buddhist text mentions a woman with tender heart wetting the master's feet with tears while worshiping his feet.[41]

In this comparison of the lives of the two masters I have concerned myself mainly with similarities, and I have by no means compared the lives of Jesus and Gautama *in toto*. This being the case, I feel that I should close the chapter with a few observations about the differences in the masters' lives.

The most significant difference hinges upon the fact that Jesus' career was abruptly ended after only two or three years. He had not yet had time to thoroughly establish his new ideas. Nor had he organized his disciples to any extent compared with Gautama. He was killed so soon after his emergence in the public eye that very few of his sermons were committed to writing or memory, again in contrast to Gautama. Jesus did not live long enough to find a ruler or principal city to support him, as did Gautama. And he was not able to leave extensive instructions for the carrying on of his mission. It is interesting to speculate on what might have been different if Jesus had been permitted to live to age eighty as was Gautama, or if the attempt that was made on the life of the young Buddha had been successful as was the case with Jesus.

A difference in the believers' understanding of the two masters follows from their very different types of deaths. Gautama lived to old age and his mission was well established, so his death was in no way tragic or monumental. As a result, I feel, the earlier event of the enlightenment became the focal one in the biographies of Buddha. Granted, the death was important and was the subject of a long text (the Mahāparinibbāna Sutta), but I would argue that the enlightenment is the ultimate event in Buddhist thought. On the other hand, Jesus' death received most of the attention. It was tragic, dramatic, and from the believer's point of view it was the focal point of salvation. The form of the Christian gospel may have arisen from very early Christian stories about the last week, especially the death and resurrection. Speaking comparatively, Christianity has no real equivalent to the enlightenment and Buddhism no counterpart to the cross and resurrection.

Another difference is that Gautama was married before his departure, whereas in the absence of any statement to the contrary it is assumed that Jesus was not.[42] This difference could have been very important, for Gautama recommended that other persons leave home and family to follow his new movement, but this injunction did not lead Christianity and Buddhism down two different paths as it might have. There are discernible reasons for this. On the one hand, the teachings of Jesus are not very different from the teaching and practices of Gautama on this point. Jesus, too, advocated leaving one's home and family if necessary—there is no saying in Buddhism any stronger on this point than Jesus' "Leave the dead to bury the dead." On the other hand, it happened that the early church, or at least a considerable part of it, adopted the notion that the priests of the new faith must be celibate. That decision effectively blurred the distinction between Israel and India on the matter of priesthood and celibacy. Meanwhile, in India and in the other countries to which Buddhism spread, the tension between family values and Buddhist monasticism was being lessened by a series of modifications in the practice of monasticism. For example, the Buddhist monks became more settled, usually near populated areas, so having a son enter the Buddhist order was not the complete severing of ties that it had been. Also, in some countries it became common for men to become monks for a few months or years and then to leave the order and marry.

It must be remembered that very different conceptions of God and afterlife shaped the lives of Gautama and Jesus. However, these divergent backgrounds did not produce the totally different masters that we might have expected and that many authors have indicated.

Concluding reflections. Returning to the distinction between a god in a spiritual body and a god in a human body (the avatar), we are now in a position to reflect upon the importance of the complex of ideas surrounding the avatar concept. Having considered the two masters' births, missions, and deaths, it is time to ask how this pattern of beliefs functioned to create major new religions in both the East and the West. Why did the concept of incarnation become so popular? How did it manage to cross cultural boundaries? What social and ideological changes help account for the rise of this new role of the human body in religion? In our search for the answers to such questions these factors are relevant.

The concept of the incarnate god draws upon *motifs common in hero legends.* Like the hero, the incarnate god is threatened during childhood by the evil powers he is destined to conquer. He has the full range of human emotions and physical limitations so that he is tempted to serve his own purposes rather than those of his heroic mission. He suffers setbacks and pain, but triumphs in the end. And of course he dies, as all mortals must. Stories of incarnate gods permit humans to identify with the god, as one would with a hero: to grow up, resist temptation, fight to conquer evil, realize the truth, and bravely face death like the god. An embodied god is more relevant to humans than a heavenly one.

The story of the incarnate god also *employs mythic motifs.* Like the gods of some ancient myths, the incarnate god journeys to face the evil powers, challenges and defeats them, and returns triumphantly to reign over a peaceful heaven. The stories of the incarnate gods also narrate the cosmic dimensions of the struggle between good and evil; but unlike the myths of cosmic conflict, the stories of the incarnate god locate the war between good and evil in a real time and place.

When his mission is accomplished and he ascends to heaven, the incarnate god leaves behind *structures that continue to embody the divine.* For example, the disciples of Gautama have the three precious jewels—Buddha, his teaching, and his order of followers. The Christians similarly have the memory of Christ, his teachings, and the church. Gods who remain in their heaven cannot establish such structures so readily.

The incarnate god is secondarily *embodied in various objects* that remain in the possession of his followers. The most important of these for the development of the Buddhist religion were the relics of Gautama's cremated body. These relics were placed in above-ground tombs (stupas), which became important pilgrimage cities. Furthermore, the stupa itself and the material objects surrounding it also became embodiments of the divine for Buddhists. The sky gods described in older myths could leave behind certain constellations, the seasonal pattern, landmarks, and other reminders of their accomplishments, but those objects are rather remote compared with the concreteness of the stupa as a place for worship or even as an object of worship. Similarly, Christians had objects sacralized by their association with the incarnate god, such as the fish, bread and wine, and especially the cross.

The incarnate god's birth and death became central to the cult. The cross, divinized by its role in the death of the incarnate god, was given the honored place at the front of the church just as the stupa was front and center in early Buddhist worship places.[43] The birth of the incarnate god became the focus for important festivals in each tradition. At Wesak[44] and Christmas, the master's coming to earth is celebrated with merry-making, gifts, special religious services, and a feeling of cosmic renewal. No such celebrations of birth and death typically occur in the cults of gods who do not become incarnate—though seasonal deities give rise to other types of birth and death festivals.

It is interesting to note that the incarnate god puts an end to animal sacrifices. Even though the Hindu and Jewish cultures made extensive use of sacrifices, the new religions that developed around the memory of the incarnate god had no place for animal sacrifices. In the Indian setting the reason given is that the taking of animal life is immoral and theologically senseless, since it is the state of the human mind that is of religious concern. Persons are now told to make offerings and give homage to the disciples who have made progress in purifying their minds.[45] In the Christian setting the symbolism of the animal sacrifice is maintained in the understanding of Christ as the lamb of God and in the eucharist, which is built upon that Christology, but the fact remains that sacrifice in its former sense is omitted in Christianity as well as Buddhism.

Why, after centuries of approaching god by means of the offering of animal life, do these religious cultures now turn away from that? I suggest that in addition to the theological reasons mentioned above there is the cultural reason that civilization was moving away from the agricultural base that made sacrifice so meaningful. Sacrifice was the religious way a herdsman or farmer related to and repaid the powers that made possible his means of livelihood. But along the Ganges in Gautama's time and around the Mediterranean in Jesus' day cities had grown to such size that many people were detached from herding and farming. Trading, manufacturing, and services had come to provide the livelihood of many people for whom sacrificing animals or firstfruits must have been perfunctory or even meaningless. Upon this stage comes the story of an incarnate god that teaches that a new kind of sacrifice is in order, a sacrifice involving the person's own mind and body rather than the fruit of his land.

The religions that developed around the incarnate god are *popular* ones in the sense of having great numbers of adherents and also in the sense of being open to all the populace. Gautama and Jesus opened salvation to all social strata. New religions usually begin with the common people, and the incarnate god who lives among the common people can open the way to meaningful religious experience for rich and poor alike.

Although the religions of the incarnate god took embodiment seriously, they concentrated their theologies upon the spirit within the body rather than upon the body itself. As I have written in the context of the Buddhist attitude toward death,[46] Buddhists were very respectful of life, but not in the same way as their Brahmanic Indian counterparts, sacrificing Hindus. The sacrificer takes life because he sees a continuity between the *animal's embodied life* and his own, but the Buddhist avoids taking life because he sees a continuity between the *animal's spirit* and his own. This distinction perhaps seems slight, but upon it rests the difference between approaching God "with blood" or "with a clean heart."

Is there a principle underlying these factors concerning the religion of the embodied god? Perhaps it is that the avatar god brings religion down to earth. Did the stories of the appearance of God on earth restore the proximity of the sacred that had been lost since the rise of the older theism? The avatar religions have kept their appeal for over two thousand years, and, as the phenomenal rise in popularity of the Guru Maharaj Ji cult has recently demonstrated, the power of the avatar formula has not diminished.

Much of the power of the two masters inheres in their message and works, which I will now discuss. Most writers on this topic have stressed the differences between the messages and approach of Gautama and Jesus, calling Gautama pessimistic, world denying, atheistic, and negative, while seeing Jesus as optimistic, world affirming, theistic, and positive. There is an element of truth in these distinctions, but they are grossly overdrawn. I shall argue the other side of the truth and call attention to the similarities in the teachings of the two masters.

II
ONE MESSAGE

The Way to a Pure Mind

In spite of their different cultural backgrounds, Gautama and Jesus gave their disciples remarkably similar instructions for the development of a pure mind. In order to establish this thesis I will present and then discuss the instructions given by each master, as these instructions have come down to us in the Buddhist and Christian written traditions.

I assume the reader has some familiarity with the four biblical Gospels, but I will review them briefly. The early Christians debated among themselves which of the many gospel accounts of Jesus' life and teachings was best. Eventually it was decided that it would be best to accept as canonical four of the accounts and reject the others, although the four accounts did not always agree in their narrative detail. The Gospel of Mark is probably the oldest. Matthew and Luke's Gospels are longer and were probably based in part on Mark's Gospel. The Gospel of John is quite different from the other three, and it is difficult to date it in relation to them. In spite of the uncertainties about specific place and date, all four Gospels were probably written by the close of the first Christian century.

For our purposes, the Gospels of Luke and Matthew are the most relevant because only those two give us an account of the sayings of Jesus on the development of what I wish to call the "pure mind." In Matthew's Gospel most of the relevant sayings are presented in the Sermon on the Mount. Luke presents many of the same sayings in his equivalent sermon, which is sometimes called the Sermon on the Plain because Luke reports that Jesus "came down with them and stood on a level place" (Luke 6:17). Many other relevant sayings occur in later chapters of Luke's Gospel, however, and a few occur in later chapters of Matthew's account.

Most of the Buddhist instructions that I will be drawing upon in this chapter are from the same Buddhist book, the Dharmapada. The many roving teachers or spiritual masters who taught out of doors along the Ganges River valley in the sixth century before Christ were expected to be able to express their messages in brief poems called *gathas,* as well as to engage in longer discourses and debates. Gautama was especially adept at composing these poems and typically ended his teaching sessions by formulating his message in such "memory verses." These little verses were very popular with the early Buddhists, and shortly after the death of Gautama some unknown disciple collected his favorite of the verses under the title "Fundamentals of Doctrine," which in Sanskrit was *Dharmapada* and in the Pali language *Dhammapada.* The Dharmapada quickly became perhaps the most popular of all Buddhist books, and for centuries many Buddhists have committed part or all of it to memory.

There is no special order to the Dharmapada verses, except that they are very loosely organized into topical chapters. Through the centuries as Buddhism spread throughout Asia and splintered into various branches or sects, each sect had a version of the Dharmapada. Like the Sermon on the Mount, the Dharmapada has inspired literally millions of people and continues to do so.

The following discussion considers the Dharmapada and biblical sayings that deal with similar themes. The order of discussion topics is not important. What is important is the overall message of the sayings, for the two masters gave essentially the same message.

Overcome anger. The law-and-order debate may be as old as

the human race. Opinions range from the extreme position, which favors capital punishment for various crimes, to the moderate position, which follows the principle that the punishment should not be greater than the crime committed—no more than "an eye for an eye." The moderate position usually allows for self-defense against an aggressor but condemns acts of aggression. However, a quite different stance has occasionally been taken on the matter of how to deal with an aggressor. This position teaches that even if attacked one should not resort to anger or violent counterattack.

The teaching of nonviolence was extant at least as early as the sixth century before Christ. For in that century in China the traveling master of wisdom, Confucius, was asked what he thought about the maxim that one should return kindness for violence. Confucius replied that he found that teaching inappropriate, for if one returns kindness for violence, with what shall one return kindness? Confucius was a gentle, peace-loving scholar-teacher, but he could not see any wisdom in the nonviolent approach. On the contrary, he felt that it was necessary for the government to maintain the peace by treating persons fairly, which would help the people in turn respect the government.

In the same century in northern India this issue was also being debated. There, as in China and in most countries even today, the consensus of opinion was that it was a part of the responsibility of the government (headed by the king in India) to enforce the laws against violent crimes. As if to warn kings of their responsibility to provide justice, it was said that when a king died and faced judgment, as all persons must, a portion of the demerit ("sin") of all unpunished crimes committed during his reign counted against the king himself. In modern terms, this is like saying that God will hold inefficient and corrupt policemen, politicians, and judges partly responsible for the murders, rapes, and muggings committed while they are in office.

Against that background of what seems to most persons a

very reasonable, responsible position on law and justice, some of the wandering teachers who taught in parks on the outskirts of some of the thriving cities of India advocated the very different, nonviolent approach. The position of these teachers grew out of an intellectual environment that I shall call *Ganges Spirituality*. For along the Ganges River in the sixth century B.C. and even before, an ascetic spirituality was practiced that held that the ultimate goal of human existence was to achieve the liberation of the spirit from matter. The state of liberation, known in Sanskrit by such terms as nirvana and *moksha,* could be achieved only by a long, arduous spiritual struggle during which time it was especially necessary to avoid generating any personal defilement. The most defiling of all actions was to do violence to another living entity, whether human or animal. Violent actions, physical or mental, were referred to as evil *karma,* and such karma defiled one's spirit horribly.

Gautama was a representative of Ganges Spirituality and accepted the spiritual world view I have just outlined. While admitting that criminals should be justly punished by the authorities, he taught his disciples not to be the cause of any killing or injury to animals or humans. But he went well beyond that to insist that they develop their minds to the point that they would no longer harbor hatred, resentment, or even anger. This is expressed in numerous Dharmapada verses such as the following:

> "He abused me, he beat me, he defeated me,
> he robbed me,"—in those who harbour such
> thoughts hatred will never cease.
>
> "He abused me, he beat me, he defeated me,
> he robbed me,"—in those who do not harbour
> such thoughts hatred will cease.
>
> For never does hatred cease by hatred here below:
> hatred ceases by love; this is an eternal law.
>
> PDh (B) 3-5

He who does not harm any living creature,
who does not kill or take part in killing,
he, I declare, is a holy man.[1]

He who is tolerant with the intolerant, who
patiently endures punishment, who is merciful
to all creatures, he, I declare, is a holy man.

Uv 33.45-46

Victory breeds hatred, for the conquered is unhappy.
He who has given up both victory and defeat,
he, the contented, is happy.

PDh (B) 201, GDh 180

Several centuries later Jesus taught a similar ethic, which has a close Buddhist parallel.

But I say to you that hear, Love your enemies, do good to those who hate you, bless those who curse you, pray for those who abuse you. To him who strikes you on the cheek, offer the other also; and from him who takes away your coat do not withhold even your shirt. Give to every one who begs from you; and of him who takes away your goods do not ask them again. But love your enemies, and do good, and lend, expecting nothing in return; and your reward will be great, and you will be sons of the Most High; for he is kind to the ungrateful and the selfish. Be merciful, even as your Father is merciful.
Luke 6:27-30, 35-36

Conquer anger by non-anger,
conquer evil by good

Conquer stinginess by gifts,
conquer lies by truth

Speak the truth,
do not yield to anger,
give if you are asked;
by these three steps you will
come near the gods.

GDh 280-281

One Message

Both Jesus and Gautama made the point that an aggressor should be overcome by converting him to a more peaceful state of mind. This can be done only by love, not by force. "Love your enemies" means exactly the same as "Conquer anger by non-anger." I believe that Jesus was referring not to the Romans (who were considered enemies by the Jewish Zealots) but that he meant personal relationships. The context makes it clear that "love your enemies" might better be expressed in English as "love the aggressive person." "Do good to those who hate you" was Jesus' way of saying what Gautama expressed with the words "conquer evil by good." Although it goes contrary to human nature as we usually experience it, we are advised to "give" (Jesus), to "conquer stinginess by gifts" (Gautama). What was called for by both masters is strength of mind on the part of the disciples, mental composure so deep that hostile words or hostile actions directed against the disciples would not cause them to become angry or hostile themselves. As Gautama summarized the matter, "Do not yield to anger." As a result of developing such a mind, Jesus' disciples would be like God. At this point we can see the difference between Jewish monotheism and Indian polytheism, for the Buddhist saying promises that one will "go near the gods," rather than becoming a son of the Most High.

Emitting anger may seem like a pleasant release, as many psychologists point out, but according to our two masters emitting anger leads to suffering in the long run:

But I say to you that everyone who is angry with his brother shall be liable to judgment; whoever insults his brother shall be liable to the council, and whoever says, "You fool!" shall be liable to the hell of fire.	Do not emit anger, for not restraining anger causes suffering; thinking at the time that it was sweet and good, one later suffers from anger.
Matt. 5:22	GDh 283

Although both Jesus and Gautama asked their disciples to refrain from anger, the sayings just cited reflect somewhat different cultural suppositions. Jesus' saying warned the hearer that the person with an angry, untamed mind would be punished, either by the Jewish court or by God. The Buddhist saying presupposes that the listener understands the operations of karmic retribution, which maintains that the power of one's evil acts, in the form of bad karma, eventually causes a retributive justice to befall the evildoer. In the Indian understanding, it is not necessary for a god to intervene to bring about justice in the afterlife. Jesus' saying draws upon an old Jewish tradition that prohibits the public insulting of a fellow Israelite, who is referred to metaphorically as one's "brother" or "neighbor."

In the sixth century before Christ, in the time of Christ, and still today the standard reaction to the teaching of nonviolence by masters such as Jesus and Gautama is that it will not work. Yet when the history of the twentieth century is written, a good case can be made that the most important phenomenon of our times was not the landing of humans on the moon or the invention of world wars but the collapse of colonialism. (Not simply the end of the European colonialism, which had existed for a few centuries, but the downfall of the ideology that had supported colonial expansionism for as long as recorded history.) When this hypothetical history is written, it will be noted that the colonial dominoes fell rapidly after the British reluctantly granted independence to the Indian subcontinent (at the time, India and Pakistan, with Ceylon soon following). Together with economic and political factors, the reason India received her independence was not a war but Gandhi's use of nonviolence. He achieved his goal by staging hunger strikes, by enduring imprisonment without being angry at the rulers who incarcerated him, and by applying to world politics a version of the teaching advocated by the two masters we are studying. Surprisingly, Gandhi first encountered the idea of nonviolence of conquering evil with good, by reading the Sermon on the Mount as a university student in England. Later he rediscovered the concept in the Indian classics and Indian cultural fabric. After graduating from law school he went to South Africa to practice. There he was appalled to be treated as a second-class citizen, a "coloured." He began to apply nonviolence to political realities, to hatreds and abuses, to laws that required segregated buses and racial discrimination in employment.

Many years after Gandhi's earliest efforts in South Africa, a young black minister wrote a doctoral dissertation on Gandhi and the notion of nonviolent resistance. He too organized peaceful protests against discrimination. This American Gandhi, Martin Luther King, Jr., gave impetus to the long, slow process of achieving full citizenship for American blacks, and again it was done by the inspiration of the Sermon on the Mount.

Perhaps when the critics of nonviolence say that it will not work, what they correctly allude to is that the person who employs the ethic of nonviolence has no assurance that it will work easily or quickly. An attempt was made on the life of Gautama when he was beginning to teach; Jesus' commitment to nonviolence certainly did not save him from the hatred of the Jerusalem political establishment. Gandhi was felled by the violent act of one of the fellow countrymen he suffered so much to liberate. And Martin Luther King, Jr., suffered the fate that so often goes with the career of the prophet, death at an early age.

Does the ethic of nonviolence work, then? As a means of self-defense, no. As a means of transforming hatred and prejudice into understanding and peace, yes.

Do not lust. Jesus and Gautama not only condemned the heightened negative emotions such as anger and hatred, they also warned against heightened attraction emotions such as sexual lust:

You have heard it was said, "You shall not commit adultery." But I say to you that every one who

Four things come to the thoughtless man who has intercourse with another's wife: demerit,

looks at a woman lustfully has already committed adultery with her in his heart. If your right eye causes you to sin, pluck it out and throw it away; it is better that you lose one of your members than that your whole body be thrown into hell. Matt. 5:27-29	restlessness, blame and hell. GDh 270 (cf. PDh 309) He who has destroyed desires for [worldly] goods, sinfulness, the bonds of the eye of flesh, who has torn up desire by the very root, he I declare, is a [holy man]. Uv 33.68

This teaching transcends the condemnation of adultery to condemn the state of mind that gives rise to adulterous thoughts. The reason given by both masters for avoiding lustful thoughts was not that sooner or later such thoughts might lead to actual adultery but rather that the state of mind itself was considered by Jesus to be sinful and by Gautama to be demeritorious. If left unreformed, unpurified, such a state of mind will eventually lead one to the punishments of hell, both masters warned. For Gautama, hell was one of six possible places or states of existence into which a person could be reborn. If a person at the time of death had an impure mind and had generated a great deal of bad karma, that person would have to suffer in hell for a period of time according to the extent and severity of his misdeeds. Eventually the effect of the bad karma, the misdeeds, would be atoned and the person would instantly leave hell and be reborn in one of the other states of existence such as that of an animal or a human.[2] We are unclear about Jesus' concept of hell. The idea of a separate heaven and hell, one up and the other down, probably had originated in Persia and spread throughout the ancient world, including the Jewish territory along the Mediterranean. Whether or not Jesus thought of the punishment of hell as eternal or as lasting only until the coming new era is difficult to discern.

Whatever their differences in the conception of hell and the nature of the judgment process, both masters taught their disciples that anger, hatred, and lust must be overcome.

Do not be judgmental. The list of negative emotional states to be avoided also includes that of being judgmental. Both masters emphasized the dangers of this state of mind:

Judge not, that you be not judged. For with the judgment you pronounce you will be judged, and the measure you give will be the measure you get.	Investigate not the faults in others, nor what others do or do not do, but investigate your own just and unjust deeds.
Why do you see the speck that is in your brother's eye, but do not notice the log that is in your own eye? Or how can you say to your brother, "Let me take the speck out of your eye," when there is the log in your own eye? You hypocrite, first take the log out of your own eye, and then you will see clearly to take the speck out of your brother's eye. Matt. 7:1-5	The fault of another is easy to see, but that of oneself is difficult to see. A person winnows the faults of another like chaff, but conceals his own sin like a cheating gambler. GDh 271-272 (cf. PDh 50, 252)

The negative state of mind that is associated with "winnowing the faults of others" is inappropriate in the same way that anger and hatred are. Namely, such states of mind nourish the evil roots of the deep mind—Buddhist thought describes these evil roots as greed, hatred, and delusion. All three of them actively feed the judgmental thoughts of the impure mind. In addition, the further problem with the judgmental state of mind is that while one is occupied with making judgments and accusations about others, one's own house is not being put in order.

The disciple of Jesus would probably have understood the words "that you be not judged" to refer to the judgment of God. Similarly the implication in the Buddhist saying is that the person who continues to deceive himself will eventually have to face the suffering that his evil actions (karma) have created. But the wise disciple should make it a priority to take the log out of his or her own eye, to winnow his or her own chaff.

Jesus and Gautama did not overlook the practical problems that arise from judgmental behavior. One should not trust in the leadership of those who have not removed the chaff from their own lives:

He also told them a parable: "Can a blind man lead a blind man? Will they not both fall into a pit?" Luke 6:39	He who commits crimes, who uses false measures, who hurts men, or who does any other similar deeds, will by walking in this path fall into a precipice Uv 9.7

In Luke's Gospel account this verse about the leadership of the spiritually blind person is placed between the two verses cited above about not judging others. Elsewhere Gautama made the same point in different words; namely, that the foolish person loves to lead others astray, all the while remaining confident that he is on the right path.

Be content. A very important part of the teaching of the two masters concerning the path toward the pure mind is the instruction to be content with whatever comes to one. Both Jesus and Gautama spent long periods of time alone, away from regular sources of food, and they found these times of physical deprivation and uncertainty to be at the same time periods of spiritual growth. Out of this experience, they instructed their disciples to rise above typical human anxieties about food and clothing and shelter, to a higher mental state of contentment:

Therefore I tell you, do not be anxious about your life, what you shall eat or what you shall drink, nor about your body, what you shall put on. Is not life more than food, and the body more than clothing? Look at the birds of the air: they neither sow nor reap nor gather into barns, and yet your heavenly	Men who have laid up no store, who live on recognized food, who have perceived void and unconditional freedom, their path is difficult to understand, like that of birds in the air. He whose appetites are stilled, who is moderate in food, who has perceived void and unconditional freedom, his path is difficult to

Father feeds them. Are you not of more value than they? Matt. 6:25-26	understand like that of birds in the air. PDh (B) 92-93

The opposite of the state of contentment is anxiety, and in Indian thought the person who is anxious over such things as food and shelter is said to be "attached." The attached person's mind is bound to the object of his attachment, whether that be food, tobacco, money, or anything else. Gautama often instructed his disciples to be free from all material dependencies:

> A Bhixu [disciple] who is satisfied with what alms are given him, and who frets not about what is given to others, who is protected by continual passionlessness and reflection, him the gods do delight in.
> Uv 32.1[3]

> Good people walk on, whatever befall; the good do not prattle, longing for pleasure; whether touched by happiness or sorrow, wise people never appear elated or depressed.
> PDh (B) 83 (cf. GDh 226)

The point of the last verse, that one should remain even-tempered whether blamed or praised, is repeated time after time in early Buddhist writings and in Hindu texts; for example the third chapter of the Bhagavad Gita praises the "steady man" whose mind is not tossed about like a ship upon the waters. The favorite metaphor for this teaching is that words of blame or praise should run off a person like water runs off a lotus flower, for the lotus plant is oily and water repellent. Perhaps Christians would say that the saint sheds flattery and condemnation like water off a duck's back.

Jesus dealt with the theme of contentment at length in the beatitudes, which begin the Sermon on the Mount. It is difficult to know, however, just what Jesus himself meant in the beatitudes. For example, Luke records the first saying as "Blessed be *you poor,* for yours is the kindgom of God," whereas Matthew has "Blessed are *the poor in spirit,* for theirs is the kingdom of heaven." Luke's version probably means that those poor, oppressed persons in the listening crowd ("you poor") should take heart, knowing that in the coming era they will be the fortunate ones. Matthew's phrase, "poor in spirit," suggests that those persons who are humble before God will be rewarded eventually.

The Buddhist equivalent of the first beatitude reads as follows: "Let us live exceedingly happy; though there be nothing to call our own, we shall feed on happiness like the shining gods" (that is, like angels). The meaning of this is not quite the same as either Matthew's or Luke's sayings. Here, there is no expectation of a coming kingdom of God, but rather there is the resolute opinion that the *voluntarily* chosen life of poverty is ultimately superior. Such a message is expressed in other teachings of Jesus, such as those which turn on the metaphor "treasures in heaven."

Store up heavenly treasures. The person who chooses to live modestly is the happier for it, if that person uses available wealth to advantage. The Buddhist tradition has always made a distinction between material wealth and spiritual advantage. The latter is called merit, meaning the spiritual power that is generated by good moral actions (karma). An ancient Indian belief holds that when a person dies, his or her merit determines the nature of the afterlife to be enjoyed. Conversely, if a person has committed numerous evil actions, his or her demerit determines which unpleasant things await after death. To teach this concept, Buddhism used an old metaphor that expressed one's accumulation of merit in physical terms. In Iranian texts we find that the good person is welcomed to the realm of the afterlife by a beautiful young maiden, who personifies his merit, while the evil person is welcomed by an old hag, his demerit. (Complete sexists, the writers apparently never considered that a worthy woman might seek admittance to the afterlife.) Two Buddhist verses employ the same theme, but without the sexual implications of the reference to the young maiden:

One Message

> Kinsmen, friends, and well-wishers salute a man who has been long away, and returns safe from afar.
> In like manner his good works receive him who has done good, and has gone from this world to the other;—as kinsmen receive one who is dear to them on his return.
>
> PDh (B) 219-20

The editor of one version of the Dharmapada placed this verse immediately after the two I have just cited: "Lay up therefore, good works in view of the other world; for it is good works that receive beings in the other world" (Uv 5.23).

Once, while making his way from village to village, Gautama came across two old men of the priestly, Brahmin class. They recognized that Gautama was a man of wisdom and began to ask him about the afterlife. Soon they confessed to him that they were terrified of dying and wanted desperately to know what they could do to alleviate their fears. Gautama told them that the way to avoid fearing one's death was to have confidence in one's accumulation of merit, for merit is a comfort in one's old age. One should start to do meritorious works even while still young: "Men who have not led a religious life and have not laid up treasure in their youth, perish like old herons in a lake without fish" (PDh (B) 155 [cf. GDh 139a]).

It is important to note that in the last verse cited the merit that one has accumulated in the other world is referred to as a treasure. This heavenly treasure is not subject to the uncertainties of a treasure of this world. Jesus and Gautama both used this metaphor:

Sell your possessions, and give alms; provide yourselves with purses that do not grow old, with a treasure in the heavens that does not fail, where no thief approaches and no moth destroys. For where your treasure is, there will your heart be also. Luke 12:32-34 (cf. Matt. 6:19-21)	One must lay up provisions of faith; for it is not possible to deprive one of his lot of merit, and one need have no fear of the robbing of thieves. Happy are the disciples who have acquired it, and happy is the wise man when he meets with (such) a disciple. Uv 10.11

These two sayings express the same theological world view; namely, that there is an afterlife, that one's state of being in the afterlife is determined by one's moral actions, and that the wise person puts more stock in this "eternal" treasure than in worldly wealth.

Jesus also illustrated the teaching about "treasures in heaven" with parables, his most distinctive form of instruction. Gautama did not usually instruct by means of parables, but there is a trilogy of Dharmapada verses that collectively parallel the parable of the rich man who trusted too much in his barns filled with food:

And he told them a parable, saying, "The land of a rich man brought forth plentifully; and he thought to himself, 'What shall I do, for I have nowhere to store my crops?' And he said, 'I will do this: I will pull down my barns, and build larger ones; and there I will store all my grain and my goods. And I will say to my soul, Soul, you have ample goods laid up for many years; take your ease, eat, drink, be merry.' But God said to him, 'Fool! This night your soul is required of you; and the things you have prepared, whose will they be?' So is he who lays up treasure for himself, and is not rich toward God."

Luke 12:16-21

"These children are mine, these riches are mine;" with these [thoughts] is the fool disturbed. What are children and riches to one who [owns] not even himself in the other world?

It is the law of humanity that, though one acquires hundreds and thousands of worldly goods, one still falls into the power of the Lord of death.

The end of all that has been hoarded up is to be spent; the end of what has been lifted up is to be cast down; the end of meeting is separation; the end of life is death.

Uv 1.20-22

In another book of the Buddhist canon there is this saying by Gautama: "Death takes what men deem their possessions. Disciple mine, lay claim to nothing" (Sutta-nipāta 806).

Jesus told other stories illustrating the foolishness of hoarding riches while others went in need of them. The story

One Message

(Luke 16:19-31) of the rich man and Lazarus, the hungry man, makes the point that the hoarding man eventually suffered in hell while the poor Lazarus enjoyed the blessings of heaven. Similarly the story of the rich man (Mark 10:17-22 and parallels) tells how at least one rich person could not give up his riches for the sake of heavenly rewards. The Danish theologian Kierkegaard, reflecting on the meaning of this story, said that if the man had been willing to give up his wealth, to sell all that he had and give to the poor, Jesus would have returned his money to him. Presumably Kierkegaard understood Jesus to be only testing the man, to see if he was too attached to his wealth. I feel that the other sayings by Jesus are consistent with the more literal interpretation of this story—Jesus really meant for the rich man to give away his wealth to the poor and for that he would have merit (treasure) in heaven.

There are numerous Buddhist stories that tell of the heavenly rewards that have been won by acts of charity. They tell about the heavenly mansions that pious persons, after death, have found waiting for them as a result of generous acts done during their lifetimes. A typical story might tell of a woman who lived in a mansion surrounded by beautiful gardens with ponds of blue lotuses. When asked what she did to deserve such a splendid heavenly life, she explained that long ago when she lived on earth she made a flower offering, a bunch of blue lotuses, to a great monk or to the Buddha at a shrine. Her reward for this was the heavenly mansion with blue lotuses.

This exaggerated reward from a single act of merit could be referred to as a "corresponding multiple reward"[4] because the reward repays the gift in kind, and manifold. But these stories come from later Buddhism, from the effort of some Buddhist instructors to motivate the ordinary people to give gifts for the support of the monastic order as well as for their own spiritual benefit. Gautama himself would not have condoned such stories, I am convinced, nor would Jesus have been pleased with them. I suspect that Gautama would have been somewhat

73

more pleased with a story about a rich person sharing his wealth with a poor person (as opposed to a holy person), and this is surely what Jesus intended, for his teachings repeat the theme over and over. In Gautama's day the wandering mendicants who were searching for the truth and for spiritual perfection *were* the poor. Later, when Buddhist monasteries became more established and affluent, there came to be a considerable difference between giving to the poor (the village beggar) and giving to the monks. The coexistence of cathedrals and beggars has often not disturbed Christians either. In both the Christian and Buddhist traditions, acts of charity toward the "church" came to be valued out of proportion to anything that found precedent in the teachings of the masters themselves. The result has been that the original message, concerning the necessity for developing the mind toward purity, has been obscured or even lost.

The original message included the following illustration taken from everyday life. The smart person knows the difference in value between two commodities and knows how to strive toward the greater one. That basic trait of human wisdom should be applied to spiritual "treasures" as well. Here is one way this is expressed in Buddhism: "If by leaving a small pleasure one sees a great pleasure, let a wise man leave the small pleasure and look to the great" (PDh (B) 290 [cf. GDh 164]). Jesus tells several little parables such as this one which make the point his way: "The kingdom of heaven is like treasure hidden in a field, which a man found and covered up; then in his joy he goes and sells all that he has and buys that field" (Matt. 13:44). Of course there is a difference in the way Gautama and Jesus conceive of the ultimate treasure. For Jesus it might be said to be acceptance into the kingdom of God, whereas for Gautama the ultimate is nirvana, and not merely winning a heavenly mansion as described in the popular story mentioned above. A Dharmapada verse expresses the relative worth of a pleasant existence on earth *or* in a heavenly mansion (like the angels or "gods") as compared with the state of nirvana that comes when the mind is purified of all evil desires such as hatred, anger, greed, lust, and materialism: "Worldly happiness and happiness in the region of the gods is not worth the sixteenth part of the happiness [resulting] from the destruction of desires" (Uv 30.33). In Christianity this dichotomy between going to heaven and "entering" nirvanic bliss did not arise because of the different cultural presuppositions.

And now to return to a more direct discussion of the central thread that runs through the teaching of the two masters—the development of the good mind.

Light the world. It is not uncommon for people to wear a facade of purity and piety that disguises the state of their minds. This is especially dangerous when these people are in positions of political or religious leadership. Gautama was concerned over the self-righteousness of some of the Brahmins and ascetics of his day, for they were not always deserving of the high respect and privilege that Indian society gave them. Jesus was likewise concerned about the spiritual hypocrisy of the Jerusalem Jewish establishment. Here is how the two masters expressed their condemnations:

Beware of false prophets, who come to you in sheep's clothing but inwardly are ravenous wolves.	Why your ascetic's hair, fool? Why your animal-hide clothes? Your interior is a jungle, though you clean the outside!
Matt. 7:15	GDh 2 (cf. PDh 394)

Gautama has other sayings making this point:

> He who in this world; not being well controlled, deceitfully, for some interested motive, produces the incorrect idea that he is well controlled by the general appearance of his garb [lit. colour and person] no confidence must be placed in him.
> As deceiving as the colour of brass, like iron coated over with gold is he whose inside is poison, and whose outward manner is that of the elect, and who goes about in this world with a great company.
> Uv 29.11-12

Two Masters, One Message

The Buddhist editor who made the Gandhari version of the Dharmapada thought that this teaching was so important that he changed the traditional order of the chapters and verses so that the following verse came first in the book:

> Not by ascetic's hair, not by clan, and not by caste does one become a holy person (Brahmin), but he who always quiets his evil tendencies, great or small, is truly called a holy person because he has quieted them all.
>
> GDh 1

Yet the problem posed by hypocritical leaders is not insolvable. Both masters encouraged their disciples to put would-be leaders to the practical test:

For no good tree bears bad fruit, nor again does a bad tree bear good fruit; for each tree is known by its own fruit. For figs are not gathered from thorns, nor are grapes picked from a bramble bush. The good man out of the good treasure of his heart produces good, and the evil man out of his evil treasure produces evil; for out of the abundance of the heart his mouth speaks. Luke 6:43-44(cf. Matt. 7:16-20)	The fool who scorns the teaching of worthy, noble, righteous persons, depending instead on bad opinion, bears fruit to his own destruction, like a thorn. GDh 258 Whatsoever a man has done, whether it be virtuous or sinful deeds, there are none that are of little importance; they all bear some kind of fruit. Uv 9.8

It is apparent that both Jesus and Gautama were moral pragmatists. They affirmed that it makes a real difference in the world whether one speaks and acts properly or improperly. They urged their followers to associate with those who spoke and acted from wisdom rather than from bold ignorance. They believed that the council of the false leader would sooner or later reveal its true nature, and they instructed their disciples in this truth by means of the metaphor of seeds. Seeds look much alike, but when they are given a chance to grow and mature, the weeds are easily distinguished from the grain or fruit.

One Message

Because of their confidence in the listeners' ability to observe and test for themselves the wisdom of their teachings, both Gautama and Jesus shunned the use of force or "hard sell" tactics in presenting their messages. Gautama especially encouraged his disciples to try the wisdom of his teachings for themselves. The same test, applied to the teachings and morality of the false leaders, would reveal their shortcomings.

It is important to note that the metaphor of actions bearing fruit applies to both the social and personal dimensions. We have seen the social dimension, with its condemnation of those who "sow bad seeds" with their bad leadership, their angry outbursts, and their false or slanderous judgments. This social immorality was condemned directly by Gautama and pictorially by Jesus in these sayings:

Do not give dogs what is holy; and do not throw your pearls before swine, lest they trample them under foot and turn to attack you.	Ashamed of the unshameful, not ashamed of the shameful; afraid of the unfearful, unafraid of the fearful; following wrong views, they go on the wrong path.
Matt. 7:6	GDh 273

The injunction against throwing what is holy to dogs may be a warning not to bestow praise and honor upon hypocritical officials. Matthew places this immediately after the verses against being judgmental, which I interpreted above to mean that the disciple should not allow himself to get into a picky, accusative state of mind. But here the meaning may be that the disciples of Jesus should not cooperate with leaders if they are evil.

The meaning of the above Buddhist saying is much clearer. The disciple is to develop a state of mind in which he discerns what is true and who is righteous, and then give full support to these.

The personal dimension of the ethic of sowing good seeds is that the disciple should take care not to commit any immoral act, for such actions will eventually fructify to his or her dismay.

As Jesus put the matter, those who live by the sword will die by the sword. Here is the explanation given by an early Buddhist who commented upon the Dharmapada verses:

> The teaching of the wise is this, that by wisdom we preserve ourselves. The foolish ridicule it—they see, and yet do wickedly; and so by their wicked deeds they reap misfortune, as he who sows the noxious plant (reaps the same). The wicked man in his own person accumulates (receives the fruit of his) guilt; the good man reaps good fruit (merit) in his own person; and so each one for himself prepares the harvest for himself.[5]

The disciple who develops the kind of mind that sows good seed benefits both himself and others, but it is not always easy to see the social value in the life of a wandering teacher of righteousness. Once while he was making his rounds from village to village Gautama happened to pass a farmer who refused to offer him food and demanded to know what contribution Gautama made to society to justify living on alms. Gautama's reply was that whereas the farmer plowed, planted, and produced physical food, a good teacher was a spiritual plowman who nurtured the moral fiber of society. Thus, the support of the truly learned traveling teacher greatly benefits everyone. I am not aware of Jesus' ever being challenged on the matter of why he had left his home and employment to live by the charity and hospitality of people in the villages he visited. We do know that he did just that and encouraged his disciples to accept the uncertainties of the homeless life as well.

The theme of the disciplined disciple being good for society is best expressed in the metaphor of the light:

You are the light of the world. A city set on a hill cannot be hid. Nor do men light a lamp and put it under a bushel, but on a stand, and it gives light to all in the house. Let your light so shine before men, that they may see	As a lotus can grow fragrant and beautiful on top a pile of garbage along a highway; Similarly the disciples of the Buddha, who have realised the Dharma, shine forth by reason of

your good works and give glory to your Father who is in heaven.
Matt. 5:14-16

their wisdom, while common mortals are blind.
GDh 303-4

This requires the disciple to be a light to others. But one must light one's own path too:

The eye is the lamp of the body. So, if your eye is sound, your whole body will be full of light; but if your eye is not sound, your whole body will be full of darkness. If then the light in you is darkness, how great is the darkness!
Matt. 6:22-23 (cf. Luke 11:34-35)

Like a man who, having eyes and who bearing also a lamp, sees all objects, is he who has heard the law of vice and of virtue; he will become perfectly wise.
The fool who is held in bondage by his body is wrapped in darkness; they who covet worldly goods consider all other things in this same (sinful) way.
Uv 22.5, 27.5

The Buddhists tell many stories to illustrate how the man who is wrapped in ignorance is to be pitied, more so than a man physically blind. The Buddhists pictured the man of ignorance as wearing blinders. A wise person can see the consequences of his actions (for himself and others), but the spiritually blind person cannot see that evil actions will bear only bitter fruit.

In sharp contrast to the person of impure mind, who throws his praise and support to swine while at the same time neglecting to honor deserving persons, is the wise, developed disciple whose pure state of mind makes him a catalyst for that which is best in society. Jesus said: "You are the salt of the earth; but if salt has lost its taste, how shall its saltness be restored? It is no longer good for anything except to be thrown out and trodden under foot by men" (Matt. 5:13). Here we see the same theme as that expressed in the call for the disciples to sow good seeds to produce good fruit. Useless persons, not to mention outright bad ones, will be cut down or thrown out like thorn bushes or stale spices.

Jesus ends his sermon, in both Matthew's and Luke's

versions, with the illustration of the two houses. Gautama used a very similar illustration:

Every one who comes to me and hears my words and does them, I will show you what he is like: he is like a man building a house, who dug deep, and laid the foundation upon rock; and when a flood arose, the stream broke against that house, and could not shake it, because it had been well built. But he who hears and does not do them is like a man who built a house on the ground without a foundation; against which the stream broke, and immediately it fell, and the ruin of that house was great. Luke 6:47-49	With a well covered house rains cannot break through; likewise with a well guarded mind evil desires cannot break through. With a poorly covered house rains break through, likewise, with an unguarded mind evil desires break through. GDh 219-20 (cf. PDh 13-14)

The building of a well guarded, *pure mind* is said to be like the building of a good house. The work must be carefully done, with no possible way left for the breaking in of anger, violence, lust, slander, evil-doing, or other manifestations of spiritual darkness. If the mental house is in good order, the disciple will be the light of the world, the salt of the earth, the maker of peace and the bearer of good fruit.

The term "pure mind" is more Buddhist than Christian, but we have seen that many parts of Gautama's path to a pure mind were also taught by Jesus. The concept of purifying the mind provides us with an interpretive framework for a new appreciation of the ethical sayings of Jesus.

Parables

In addition to short, pithy sayings such as those of the Sermon on the Mount, the masters also illustrated their messages with longer stories, parables, comparing spiritual truths with truths of everyday life. I will now discuss the role of parables in the two masters' illustrations and point out some similarities here as well.

It was the distinctive style of Jesus to illustrate his teachings by suggesting a likeness from ordinary life. Such likenesses, which we call parables, could be long and complex, such as the story of the prodigal son, or as short as the question, Can a blind man lead a blind man?

Gautama used similes, metaphors, and parables almost as much as Jesus.[6] Let us consider some parables that are found in both the Buddhist and Christian traditions, beginning with the story of a sower and his various fields:

"Listen! A sower went out to sow. And as he sowed, some seed fell along the path, and the birds came and devoured it. Other seed fell on rocky ground, where it had not much soil, and immediately it sprang up, since it had no depth of soil; and when the sun rose it was scorched, and since it had no root it withered away. Other seed fell among thorns and the thorns grew up and choked it, and it yielded no grain. And other seeds fell into good soil and brought forth grain, growing up and increasing and yielding thirtyfold and sixtyfold and a hundredfold."

"The sower sows the word. And these are the ones along the path, where the word is sown; when they hear, Satan immediately comes and takes away the word which is sown in them. And these in like manner are the ones sown

"Now what think you, headman? Suppose a yeoman farmer here has three fields, one excellent, one moderate, and one poor, hard, saltish, of bad soil. Now what think you, headman? When that yeoman farmer wants to sow his seed, which field would he sow first . . . ?

"That yeoman farmer, lord, wishing to sow his seed, would first sow the excellent field, and having done so he would sow the moderate one. Having so done he might and might not sow the field that is poor . . .

"Well, headman, just like that excellent field are my ordained disciples, both men and women. I teach them the Norm that is upon rocky ground, who, when they hear the word, immediately receive it with joy; and they have no root in themselves, but endure for a while; then, when tribulation or persecution arises . . . , immediately they fall away. And others are the ones sown among thorns; they are those who hear the word, but the cares of the world, and the delight in riches, and the desire for other things, enter in and choke the word, and it proves unfruitful. But those that were sown upon the good soil are the ones who hear the word and accept it and bear fruit, thirtyfold and sixtyfold and a hundredfold."

Mark 4:3-8; 14-20

lovely in its beginning, lovely in its middle and lovely in its ending, both in spirit and in letter. . . . Because, headman, these people abide with me for their island, with me for their cave of shelter, me for their stronghold, me for their refuge.

"Then, headman, just like that moderate field are my lay-disciples, both men and women. I teach them the Norm that is lovely in its beginning. . . .

"Then, headman, just like that field that is poor, hard, saltish, of bad soil, are my [the] wandering recluses and brahmins that hold other views than mine. To them also I teach the Norm that is lovely. . . . Because if so be they understand but a single sentence of it, that would be to their profit and happiness for many a long day."

Kindred Sayings, iv.221-22

The illustration is the same in both stories (a farmer encounters different kinds of fields while sowing seed), but the point derived from that illustration varies. In the Buddhist text the point is that the master encounters diverse audiences in his teaching mission. According to Mark's Gospel, Jesus interpreted his own parable in this instance for the sake of his disciples.[7] In this interpretation, the point of the parable is that there are many kinds of disciples, some of whom provide great return while others fall away because of the wiles of Satan or the shallowness of their dedication. That is, both Jesus and Gautama compared the act of teaching with sowing seed and the abilities of the hearers with various fields.

Another parable of Jesus' drawn from agriculture also has a Buddhist parallel:

And he said, "The kingdom of God is as if a man should scatter seed upon the ground, and should sleep and rise night and day, and the seed should sprout and grow, he knows not how. The earth produces of itself, first the blade, then he ear, then the full grain in the ear. But when the grain is ripe, at once he puts in the sickle, because the harvest has come."

Mark 4:26-29

Herein, monks, the yeoman farmer gets his field well ploughed... puts in his seed... lets the water in and turns it off very quickly. These are his three urgent duties. Now monks, that yeoman farmer has no such magic power or authority as to say: "Let my crops spring up today. Tomorrow let them ear. On the following day let them ripen." No! It is just the due season which makes them do this.

Now the monk has no such magic power or authority as to say: "Today: let my mind be released from the āsavas [impurities] without grasping, or tomorrow, or the day following."

Gradual Sayings 1.219

Gautama compares a disciple to a farmer, saying that each must do three things, then wait for the "crop" to mature of its own good time. Jesus says that the kingdom of God (on earth?) can be started, like seeds, but it must develop on its own until the time of harvest. The two masters are telling their disciples to work hard and quickly, but also to be patient, like a farmer. The disciples of Jesus must patiently await the coming of God's kingdom, whereas Gautama's disciples must patiently await their mental purification. Again, the differences between the two masters hinge upon their theological divergences.

A Buddhist parable of the poor son occurs in the fourth chapter of the most popular of all the early Mahayana scriptures, the "Lotus of the True Law." In this chapter of the

Lotus Sutra, as it is commonly called, the Buddha has just finished telling one of his outstanding disciples that disciples too can become Buddhas in a future time.[8] Excited by this new promise that disciples could achieve supreme enlightenment as well as nirvanic bliss, three other of Buddha's leading disciples approached him respectfully and told a parable that parallels the biblical parable of the prodigal son. I assume that the reader is familiar with the prodigal son story as found in Luke (15:11-32), and I shall summarize the long Buddhist story,[9] which the disciples tell to illustrate their joy at learning that they are "sons" of the Buddha.

A certain young man was seduced away from his father by foolish people and wandered in search of pleasures. He soon became destitute and was reduced to begging. Meanwhile, his father had left his home to go from place to place in search of his son, whom he greatly missed. Eventually the father settled in a new town and became a rich merchant and banker, living in splendor as the lord of a large estate. The destitute son happened to come to his father's house, but he did not recognize his father and left, fearful of a man who lived in such opulence. The father recognized his son, however, and sent servants to apprehend the fleeing beggar. Without revealing their relationship, the rich man offered his son food in exchange for performing menial tasks on the estate. The father watched the son's progressive return to health and promoted him as he deserved, until at the old man's death some years later the son had risen to the rank of foreman. The old man called friends to his deathbed and announced his will, bequeathing all his wealth to his foreman, whom he disclosed as his son. The son was overcome with joy and gratitude, remembering his former miseries and contrasting them with the great fortune that had been so unexpectedly given to him.

The content of the story is quite similar to the parable of the prodigal son found in Luke. But the context is somewhat different, for according to Luke's editing, Jesus told his story as one of several illustrations that God is most concerned about his "lost" sons. God is said to rejoice over the return of a lost one like a shepherd who has found a lost sheep, a woman a lost coin, or a father a lost son. So far, the point of the parable is not far removed from the use made of it by Buddha's disciples, who tell the story to illustrate their own gratitude for being given (the promise of) enlightenment when they neither deserved nor expected it. In their words: "We are astonished and amazed, and deem it a great gain, O Lord, that to-day, on a sudden, we have heard from the Lord a voice such as we never heard before, an incomparable jewel. We had not sought, nor searched, nor expected, nor required so magnificent a jewel."[10] Thus, the Buddhist story is told from the recipient's point of view and the emphasis is on the surprise and thrill of being made an heir, a "son," and receiving the ultimate (spiritual) treasure.

The inclusion of a second son in Luke's story makes the parable fit into the New Testament context, for the complaint of the older son is implicitly like the murmuring of the pharisees and scribes (Luke 15:2). There is no second son in the Buddhist parable, nor is there any equivalent of the "pharisees and scribes" that the older son may represent.[11]

In summary, the two masters teach in comparisons, whether brief or long, involved narratives. In any form these comparisons as used by the masters seem especially capable of influencing the moral lives of many of those they encountered. It remains true that parables play a bigger role in the teaching style of Jesus, but Gautama also employed this pedagogical device. Gautama's favorite teaching device, on the other hand, was a brief poetic form known in India as a gatha, as previously mentioned. He seems to have been adept at summarizing a long prose answer with a brief verse.

The verbal instruction of the two teachers was punctuated by miracles, to which I now turn.

Miracles

Jesus' miracles are well known. A large portion of the Gospel narratives, especially that of Mark, is devoted to them. Some scholars have pointed out that in the Gospel of John especially there is a hint to the readers that the miracles, though genuine and important, are secondary, existing for those who are not able to have faith in Christ apart from "signs." In spite of this possible exception, I think it accurate to say that the early Christians, including the Gospel writers, considered the miracles an authentic, essential part of the mission of Jesus. And Paul, the first Christian preacher and theologian of record, puts all his theological eggs in one basket—faith in the miraculous resurrection of Jesus from the dead.

It is true that in recent years Christians have not emphasized the importance of miracles, pointing instead to some of the teachings of Jesus, but through the Christian centuries the miracles of Jesus have been recounted, painted, and dramatized countless times.

In comparison with Christian thought, Buddhist writings at first seem almost devoid of miracles. Modern Buddhists writing about Gautama for non-Buddhist readers seldom mention anything miraculous in his life. But the art in Buddhist temples and the stories traditionally told about the rewards of merit reveal the considerable role that the miraculous actually plays in Buddhism as well as in Christianity. Furthermore, when one turns to the traditional biographies of Gautama's life, especially the long ones written well after his death, one finds miraculous details narrated on practically every page.

Even in our earliest accounts of the life of Gautama, those biographical passages contained here and there in the canon, there is considerable mention made of miracles. Gautama, like Jesus, performed miracles from time to time, and also certain miraculous happenings, such as trees blooming out of season or jewels appearing suddenly from the ground, surrounded Gautama at times. It is a difficult scholarly problem to decide which of the miracles reported in the Buddhist texts were part of the earliest record (or, put in a more radical way, to know if Gautama actually performed any miracles). Were there really any miraculous events surrounding his career? The same questions are raised about the life and miracles of Jesus.

Leaving aside any question of the authenticity of the miracles, I will compare those miracles which the Buddhist and Christian traditions allege to have been performed by the masters or one of their disciples. In comparing the miracles of the two masters I wish to impose a distinction between "practical miracles" and "impressive miracles." (This distinction is not found in the texts themselves.)

Practical miracles. To begin, there are the miracles that the masters perform for very practical purposes. The most common of these in the Christian narratives is healing. In the course of narrating other events in the life of Jesus, the writers almost casually mention that on a particular occasion Jesus also healed people. For example, in his introduction to the Sermon on the Mount, Luke mentioned that Jesus healed the people's diseases and cast out the unclean spirits from them. This hints at a distinction that is made in the Gospels, implicitly at least, between physical and "spiritual" (caused by evil spirits) illnesses. Jesus healed both kinds. There is no evidence that he confined himself to any one method, but we know that he sometimes healed by rubbing some spittle from his mouth on the sick person. This restored sight, as in the story of the blind man of Bethsaida (Mark 8:22-26).

There is at least one mention of a similar healing by Gautama. It is said that Gautama's stepmother developed cataracts on her eyes as a result of the tears of grief she had shed over his leaving home. (Implausible as this may be medically, the sentiments thus expressed are uncomfortably familiar to many. The character Momma in the contemporary cartoon of the same name by Mell Lazarus is completely at home with that kind of statement.) When Gautama returned to his home city he performed a great miracle (which is called "the twin" for reasons I will describe later). Gautama's wife took some of the water that was miraculously issuing from the upper half of Gautama's body, washed the blind woman's eyes, and sight was restored. This miracle is said to have happened because of the *power* of the Buddha.[12] The word *power* here refers to the spiritual potency that he had accumulated during his many virtuous lives. If the passage had been written from the perspective of a Jew or Christian it would have said the miracle was done by the power of God (or the Holy Spirit, or the finger of God). The difference in theological perspectives is again evident. What the Buddhists attribute to the power of a perfected human mind or to karmic virtue, the biblical perspective attributes to the power of God working through humans or through historical events. The results are similar, but the explanations of these results are not.

While healing miracles do not play a very large role in the story of Gautama, the notion that the master's mission includes the healing of the sick exists in Buddhism as well as Christianity. A commentary upon a Dharmapada verse tells the story of Gautama's tending the putrid sores of a leprous monk, and then adds this explanation, which I will cite alongside the quotation from the book of Isaiah that Jesus read in the temple at the start of his ministry:

The Spirit of the Lord is upon me, because he has anointed me to preach good news to the poor. He has sent me to proclaim release to the captives and recovering of sight to the blind, to set at liberty those who are oppressed, to proclaim the acceptable year of the Lord. Luke 4:18-19	The purpose of Tathagata [Buddha] in coming into the world is to befriend those poor and helpless and unprotected—to nourish those in bodily affliction . . . to help the impoverished, the orphan, and the aged. . . .[13]

Just as the Gospel accounts frequently mention that Jesus went about preaching, healing the sick, and exorcising demons, one Buddhist biography says the following of Gautama:

> When the Exalted One enters a city, horses neigh, elephants trumpet, peacocks dance, cuckoos call, musical instruments sound without anyone playing them, and jewels rattle in their caskets. At

that moment the blind recover their sight, the deaf their hearing, and the insane their reason. The poisoned become rid of poison. The unbelieving and those slow of faith now become convinced.[14]

The difference between the two masters is not in the concept of what masters accomplish but in the way they accomplish it. Jesus healed actively, whereas the cures happened around Gautama without his being actively involved.

There are other kinds of practical miracles that occur in the Buddhist and Christian accounts. Jesus' *multiplication miracles* are examples of one such type. Mark's account says that on one occasion Jesus miraculously multiplied food to feed four thousand and on another occasion five thousand.

As was the case with healing miracles, multiplication miracles do not play as large a role in Buddhism, but they are not absent. A commentator's introduction to one of the stories of Gautama's former lives relates a series of multiplication miracles that had the practical purpose of converting a miser. Since the story is interesting and also typical of later Buddhist stories, I shall retell it at length.

There was a very rich but miserly man who could not stand to give any of his wealth away to help others, nor could he bring himself to use his wealth for his own happiness. One day he saw a peasant enjoying a piece of cake. Normally the rich man ate only the cheapest food and hoarded his foodstuffs, but the craving for a sweet overcame him and he asked his wife to get the honey, flour, and oil needed to make him a small cake. To avoid sharing with even his children or servants, he and his wife crept upstairs where she could cook in secret. From a great distance Gautama discerned what the miser was doing and undertook to change his heart. Gautama sent one of his disciples to do this, giving the disciple the power to multiply food. The disciple flew through the air—a common miracle of holy men in Indian stories—and suddenly appeared at the miser's secret baking session. The miser was deeply upset at the sight of a beggar, and he rudely ordered him to go away. The monk persisted, so finally to get rid of him the miser ordered his wife to bake a very small cake for the monk. She tried to do this, but the cake grew quite large. The miser refused to give away such a big cake and himself undertook to bake a tiny cake. It too became huge, and this happened several times. The miser gave up and decided to give one cake away, even though they were large. But he could not get the cakes apart. When the miser reached the point of exasperation and exhaustion, his personality changed for the better and he listened to the monk's sermon on generosity. The monk magically transported the couple to the park where Gautama and five hundred of his disciples were waiting to be fed. The few cakes miraculously fed all five hundred, and there were some left over. The miserly couple, both impressed and converted, returned home and began the pleasurable task of distributing to those in need.[15]

From time to time nature bends her rules a bit for the sake of the masters. This is particularly the case in the stories of Gautama, where trees punctuated the master's life with miraculous behavior. All four of the principal events in the life of Gautama occurred in a grove of trees, and in the later stories, at least, these trees perform miracles. At his birth a tree miraculously bent down a branch for Queen Maya to hold while delivering. At his enlightenment under a tree, flowers of many types rained down all around him.[16] At his first sermon in the park near Benares, a throne seat miraculously appeared; and at his death the trees suddenly blossomed. There were other miraculous trees, such as the fruit trees that sprang up instantly when Gautama planted an amra fruit pit, so that he could eat amra fruit and recover from "sickness and colic."[17] This account of the fruit tree that suddenly grew and bore fruit is in sharp contrast with the fig tree that quickly withered after Jesus cursed it for not having figs. The two stories, though so different, both establish the master's power, even over nature.

There are other miracles that the masters do not have in common. For example, the Buddhist texts quite often refer to the magic flight of a holy man, whether Gautama or one of his disciples. For example, it is said that when Gautama was traveling toward Benares to give his first sermon he came to the Ganges without any means to pay the ferryman for passage. When the ferryman refused to take him, Gautama merely went across above the water by the power of his great merit.

On the other hand, Jesus is said to have worked the miracle of raising the dead, which had precedents in Judaism. This is the ultimate in healing miracles, and was performed by Jesus for the same motivations of compassion and concern that lay behind his healings.

Miracles of faith. Neither master wished to be considered a mere magician or miracle worker. Especially in the Gospel of Mark it would seem that Jesus regularly instructed those who witnessed his miraculous healings not to tell others of the incident. Some scholars have seen this as part of an overall plan to maintain a "messianic secret," to keep Jesus' identity as the Christ hidden for a while at least. I am more inclined to think that Jesus wanted to avoid the image of a traveling miracle worker—he was not successful at avoiding this image, it would seem. Gautama refused to engage in displays of magical powers. He instructed his disciples neither to perform magic for the sake of impressing a crowd nor to attend such a magic show. Here is the way he stated the matter in response to a request to send a disciple to convert some persons with the help of a miracle: "The Blessed One replied: Kevaddha, I do not teach the Law to bhikkhus in that way: [saying] 'Come, bhikkhus, work a marvel of supernormal power higher than the human state for the white-clothed laity.'"[18] Gautama went on to explain that he knew of three different kinds of miracles. First he named miracles that are usually called "magical powers." These include such things as walking on water, flying through the air, passing through walls and closed doors, and going to visit the heavenly realm. A second kind of miracle is that of seemingly supernormal mental abilities, such as the ability to read minds. Gautama felt these two kinds of miracles were well within the realm of possibility for the person with a perfected mind, but they were not to be used to impress people. A third kind of miracle is the "miracle of instruction," that is, the practice of teaching people the right mode of behaving, which will work wonders in their lives. We can see that in this passage Gautama used a teaching device which was a favorite with him, as the parable was with Jesus. Gautama liked to instruct by reinterpreting a word or phrase to suit his purpose. In this case he said to the layman who requested a miracle that his disciples would indeed give the people a miracle, the "miracle" of the truth.

Similarly, Jesus refused to give a miracle ("sign") when asked, and instead pointed out that the history of the Jewish people provides many "signs" of how God expects his people to behave. This twist of meaning and the intended result is very much like that of Gautama's.

In spite of the prohibition on the part of both Jesus and Gautama against "impressive miracles," such miracles did occur according to the stories we have, especially in the later Buddhist stories. Gautama and his disciples did walk over water, fly through the air, read minds, and so forth. Let me give some examples of this.

When Gautama was just beginning his teaching career, he used numerous miracles to impress and convert an ascetic leader (Kassapa) and his five hundred disciples. For example, when a flood innundated an entire region, Gautama thought to himself, "Suppose I made the waters stand back all round so that I could walk in between on dry ground?"[19] He did that, and Kassapa was so impressed that he finally gave in and became a disciple of Gautama's.[20]

The most famous of Gautama's miracles is the "twin miracle," which he performed on several occasions, including that of his visit to his hometown after his enlightenment. He also performed it to establish his superiority over several rival ascetics—like Elijah's miracle before the priests of Baal on Mount Carmel. It is called the twin miracle in the texts because the Buddha manifests heat and cold water at the same time,

One Message

while hovering above the ground in a state of levitation!

> Then the Exalted One standing in the air at the height of a palm-tree performed various and diverse miracles of double appearance. The lower part of his body would be in flames, while from the upper part there streamed five-hundred jets of cold water. While the upper part of his body was in flames, five-hundred jets of cold water streamed from the lower part.[21]

Returning to the consideration of Buddhist miracles intended to impress and thereby convert, I should mention the way in which Gautama converted the bandit "Finger-garland" (which I discussed in comparison with Jesus' conversion of one of the two thieves crucified with him). Gautama worked a miracle in order to gain the bandit's attention and confidence. Gautama managed to levitate a few feet off the ground and then to move just fast enough to stay barely ahead of the pursuing bandit.

Another levitation miracle that is common in Indian literature, not just Buddhist literature, is that of walking on water, or walking above water. Gautama used this miracle himself occasionally, but there is a Buddhist story that shows that a disciple can also walk on water if his power of concentration is strong. The story has a close biblical parallel:

And Peter answered him, "Lord, if it is you, bid me come to you on the water." He said, "Come," so Peter got out of the boat and walked on the water and came to Jesus; but when he saw the wind, he was afraid, and beginning to sink he cried out, "Lord, save me." Jesus immediately reached out his hand and caught him, saying to him, "O man of little faith, why did you doubt?" And when they got into the boat, the wind ceased. And those in the

He arrived at the bank of the river Aciravatī in the evening. As the ferryman had drawn the boat up on the beach, and had gone to listen to the Doctrine, the disciple saw no boat at the ferry, so finding joy in making Buddha the object of his meditation he walked across the river. His feet did not sink in the water. He went as though on the surface of the earth, but when he reached the middle he saw waves. Then his joy in meditating on the Buddha

boat worshiped him, saying, "Truly you are the Son of God." Matt. 14:28-33	grew small, and his feet began to sink. But making firm his joy in meditating on the Buddha, he went on the surface of the water, entered the Jetavana, saluted the Teacher, and sat on one side. (Commentary to) Jataka 190[22]

In both passages a disciple walked on the water by means of faith in, or concentration upon, the master. In each case the disciple began to sink when fear disturbed his meditation. Peter's concentration is disturbed by the wind on the water, and the Buddhist disciple's by the waves. In each case the disciple's state of levitation is restored when his concentration upon and confidence in the master is restored. In addition to these remarkable similarities, there are parallels in details of the story such as the mention of a boat and the occasion of a sermon by the master. A difference in the stories involves the fact that in the biblical account Jesus himself has just walked upon the water, as reported also by Mark and John, whereas Gautama does not walk over the river on this particular occasion.

The idea that miracles can be performed by the power of faith is also common to the two traditions. For example the Buddhist saying about concentration—*samadhi* (samādhi), a meditational state of mind—being able to cut through or destroy a mountain may be compared with the saying of Jesus about the similar power of faith.

For truly, I say to you, if you have faith as a grain of mustard seed, you will say to this mountain, "Move from here to there," and it will move; and nothing will be impossible to you. Matt. 17:20	Monks, with six things endowed, a monk may cleave the mountain-king, Himalaya. . . . What six? Herein, monks, a monk is skilled in the attainment of . . . , in maintaining . . . , emerging from . . . , in the weal of . . . , in the resolve for . . . , in the range of concentration. *Gradual Sayings* iii.222

One Message

It is in comparing passages like these, which make a similar point, that we can see the difference between the theological and karmic perspective. I would understand the biblical passage to mean that the person who completely trusts in God will find that God will do great things through him. The Buddhist passage, on the other hand, has no theological overtones and means that the person who has perfected his mind to such a degree that he can completely concentrate his mental powers upon one thing can achieve marvels. Both masters indulge in the hyperbole of moving or cleaving mountains in order to affirm the incredible and extraordinary power of the mind to effect its purposes by *willing,* but they do this from different perspectives.

Masters use miracles. That much is clear from the stories told about the life and mission of Gautama and Jesus. The details about their actual use of miracles and their instructions to the disciples concerning them is not so clear, however. Jesus attributes miracles to God and seems to expect that his followers will be able to work miracles too. Gautama, on the other hand, is confident that his disciples can work miracles because of their mental perfections, but he instructs them not to do so, for he wishes his message to have the limelight. This difference in strategy resulted in a difference in the two traditions, with Christians eager for displays of the "working of the spirit" and Buddhist saints on guard lest they give the impression of being miracle workers—displaying magical powers is cause for dismissal from the order of monks. This difference was not an absolute one, however, for through the centuries Christians had difficulty in maintaining their miraculous powers and Buddhists could not resist attributing something of the miraculous to their saints and especially to the auspicious chants.

The similarities of ethical instruction, in the metaphors of instruction and in miracles, suggest that in the sphere of ethics what we have is *two masters, one message.*

95

III
THE QUESTION OF BORROWING

One Hundred Years of Scholarship on the Question

Did one master borrow from the other? Is that why there are so many sayings and stories that are similar?

This question was not even seriously considered for the first eighteen hundred years of Christianity's existence, but when European scholars of the mid-nineteenth century became more informed about Buddhism, as a by-product of the centuries of European rule in Asia, the issue did engage a few scholars. They first asked themselves the obvious question: Which came first, Buddhism or Christianity? The answer to that seemed simple, for Gautama had been dead over four hundred years before Jesus was born. But the dating problem is not always so easily solved, since some of the Buddhist stories and sayings were not actually written down until well after the birth of Jesus; so perhaps the borrowing was on the part of the Buddhists rather than the Christians. This remains a possibility, but for the most part the scholarly tendency has been to look upon the Buddhist texts as earlier and therefore to look with a suspicious eye to those biblical passages which seem curiously parallel to them.

It was almost exactly a century ago when a few Christian scholars became excited about the possibility that Buddhist stories and doctrines may have influenced portions of the New Testament and some of the Christian writings of the second century. Before I discuss some of the recent historical findings and develop my own hypothesis, I wish to review the work of scholars who have devoted book-length studies to the question of influence. I shall confine myself to the major efforts to prove that there was indeed some Buddhist influence on the New Testament itself. In some instances I find the scholars' motives as interesting as their conclusions, so I will discuss these as well.

Ernest de Bunsen. One of the earliest proponents of the thesis of Buddhist influence on the New Testament was the Dutch scholar Ernest de Bunsen, whose book, *The Angel-Messiah of Buddhists, Essenes, and Christians,* appeared in 1880.[1] De Bunsen's thesis is that a group of Jews foreign to Palestine introduced into some Jewish circles and eventually into Christianity the concept of an "angel-messiah." He argued that the Essenes—members of a Jewish sect in Jesus' day—were the locus of this new, Eastern understanding of the coming messiah as an angel who comes from above.

De Bunsen argues that Jesus at first tried to conceal the fact that he was the messiah because he did not accept the Essenes' understanding of the messiah as an angel-messiah, a god on earth. Perhaps, de Bunsen speculates, Jesus planned to set the record straight and deny the Essenic understanding of messiah-ship when his movement succeeded and he had risen to power as leader of a spiritual kingdom within Judaism.[2]

Thus, in his section on Jesus and the nature of the messiah, de Bunsen admits that his own position, and his motivation for writing the book, may be inferred from this belief: the conception of the angel-messiah, which he traces back to Buddhist sources, is a false conception, a heresy within early Christianity, as de Bunsen conceives it. He understands Jesus

> as a chosen instrument of that saving power by which God had anointed him or made him a Christ, as the man who denounced the law and the Prophets for having prophesied about the future coming, whilst not pointing to the present working of God's spirit in the flesh—in short, as the anointed Man, not as an anointed Angel, Jesus was and is the Christ.[3]

> The kingdom of heaven preached by Jesus is not the kingdom of the Angel-Messiah as preached by John the Baptist or Essene. The New

Covenant is the covenant of a good conscience with God. Herein lies the efficacy of Christ's redemption, the world-conquering power of Christianity.[4]

De Bunsen felt that the tradition that Luke followed in his narrative did not interpret Jesus as an angel-messiah, but Luke himself seems to allude to this understanding in his interpolations. For example, Luke attributes words of Jesus to the Wisdom of God, who had sent the Prophets in all ages.[5]

Of course the discovery of the Essenic texts at Qumran renders de Bunsen's speculations obsolete, but there is in his book this idea of possible value: The Christian understanding of Christ as God-come-down-in-human-form is more Indian than Hebrew and may well have arisen in Christian (or Jewish sectarian) circles under indirect influence from India.

R. Seydel. In 1882 there appeared in Germany a work by Seydel that made a strong argument for Buddhist influence on the New Testament.[6] Seydel's best contribution was to draw attention to the remarkable similarity between Gospel accounts of Jesus' infancy and the biography of the Buddha according to the Lalitavistara, but he also pointed out various other Christian texts that he thought were Buddhist influenced. His weakness was that he paid little attention to the dates of his Buddhist texts and this enabled his critics to dismiss him by saying that the influence, if it existed at all, must have been that of Christianity upon Buddhism. His lasting contribution is that he focused attention upon the Lalitavistara biography, the stories of which are thought by many to have a definite influence on some second-century Christian gospels; but more on that subject later.

Van Eysinga, Pfleiderer, and Schmiedel. In 1901 a Dutch scholar, van den Bergh van Eysinga, set forth many Buddhist-Christian parallel texts and was especially helpful in calling attention to the parallels between late Buddhist biographies and some post-canonical Christian writings. Otto Pfleiderer's writing (1906) accepted Buddhism as one of the several religions synthesized into early Christianity, and he believed Luke's infancy narrative must have been influenced by Buddhism. In the same year, Otto Schmiedel wrote in acceptance of the Buddhist influence thesis for parts of Luke, John, and some apocryphal narratives.[7]

Arthur Lillie. The author who went farthest in seeing Buddhist influence upon early Christianity was probably Arthur Lillie. He became fascinated with Indian religion, especially Shaivism, while a civil servant in India, and wrote *Buddhism in Christianity* and *India in Primitive Christianity* (1909). In the latter book, he recounted the story of Buddha's life in such a way as to emphasize its similarity with the Lucan infancy narrative. Lillie was impressed by these parallel motifs: the "virgin" conception of Maya and Mary, the annunciation by angels, the star in the East that indicates the birth, the occurrence of the birth while the mother is on a journey, the tree that bends down to aid the mother, the kings who come to venerate the baby, the old sage who predicts his future, the idols that bow down to the boy when he is taken to the temple (an Egyptian temple in the case of Jesus), and the writing teacher who is astounded by the boy's knowledge of the alphabet and its secret interpretations.

To display so many parallels, Lillie had to draw on a variety of Buddhist texts preserved in schools of Buddhism as divergent as Sri Lanka and China and, on the other hand, for his best parallels in the Christian accounts, he cited passages from the apocryphal gospels.

It was this kind of scholarship (by Seydel and Lillie), paying little attention to dates, schools of thought, geography, or textual criticism, which seriously damaged the credibility of the hypothesis of Buddhist influence on the New Testament. However, the following two scholars, whose knowledge of Buddhism was deeper, were much more cautious in accepting the idea of historical influence on the New Testament, and as a result their work has a lasting value.

Albert Edmunds. The work of Albert Edmunds remains perhaps the most helpful of all scholarship on the question.

His articles on "Gospel Parallels from Pali Texts" appeared in the journal *The Open Court* in 1900 and 1901; and then in 1902, they were published with more extensive notes in a two-volume work entitled *Buddhist and Christian Gospels*. This work went through many editions during the next thirty years and came to include valuable notes on the Chinese texts by M. Anesaki.

Edmunds' arrangement of his material under the term "parallel" passages and his scattered suggestions that certain of the passages were "literary parallels" led the reader to believe (mistakenly) that Edmunds was arguing that Buddhism heavily influenced the New Testament. Many of his contemporary reviewers misinterpreted him in this way and promptly rejected his work.

But Edmunds was a painstaking scholar who took the trouble to learn the Pali language well; and this knowledge, combined with his good command of Greek and the Christian writings, make his early work still the best, after over seventy years.

Why did he work so long and passionately on this question, even though his finances were depleted by it and his colleagues were critical? There is this very interesting admission hidden away in the middle of the second volume in the context of a discussion of whether or not Christianity in turn may have influenced later Mahayana Buddhism:

> I believe myself that Buddhism and Christianity, whether historically connected or not, are two parts of one great spiritual movement—one cosmic upheaval of the human soul, which burst open a crater in India five hundred years before Christ and a second and greater one in Palestine at the Christian Advent. Whether the lava which the twain ejected ever met in early times or not is of little moment: it came from the same fount of fire. And now, over the whole planet, the two have assuredly met, and the shaping of the religion of the future lies largely in their hands.[8]

This sudden intrusion of Edmunds' personality into his work gives us insight into his methodology and criteria for text selection. His purpose was to present the true religion, with each of its tenets proof-texted from its two great exponents, Gautama and Jesus. He never handled a set of parallel texts in such a way as to suggest a negative value judgment on either Gautama or Jesus, nor did it bother him to consider as "parallel" two texts that have absolutely nothing in common except a similar theological intent.

The question of historical influence is secondary to Edmunds' theological interest. That is why he gives the reader no help, or very little help, in distinguishing which parallels are candidates for Buddhist influence and which are merely parallel in intent. Presumably, he does not want to risk making historical judgments lest he somehow jeopardize the theological impact of his work. Also, to be fair, we must see his confidence in Buddhism and Christianity as future global religions in its turn-of-the-century context, when Christian missionary expectations were high and the demise of the colonial era was not yet apparent.

Actually, Edmunds included among his parallels stories from the two traditions that manifest any one of these: similar plot; similar spiritual experiences on the part of Gautama and Jesus; similar reactions on the part of the hearers; similar views of the gods, angels, or other religious belief; or similar wordings. His failure to at least distinguish these various similarities weakened the presentation of his "parallel" texts. These weaknesses kept Edmunds' work from being appreciated either as phenomenology or as a historical study.

In some of Edmunds' articles and here and there in his book, he does present parallel passages that he feels demonstrate Buddhist influence on the New Testament. Among the examples of passages in the New Testament that he considered to have been inspired by Buddhism are the following: several parts of Luke's infancy narrative, the story of the Penitent Thief, the idea of plucking out an offending eye, the story of the temptation of Jesus (he also considered the possibility of

Zoroastrian influence on this particular story), and especially the two unidentified scriptural citations in John.

Edmunds argued very strongly along the following lines that there had been Buddhist influence on the two passages in John. Concerning the statement in John 7:38 that "as the scripture has said, 'Out of his heart shall flow rivers of living water,'" Edmunds points out that whereas there is no such Hebrew scriptural passage, there is in fact a Buddhist one, which says of the Buddha, "and from his lower body proceeds a torrent of water."[9] Similarly, there is no biblical precedent for the statement in John 12:34 by the crowd that they have heard that the Christ will remain forever (literally, unto the aeon), but in one place the Buddha explains that if he wanted to, he could remain for the aeon.[10] Though in each of the Buddhist passages there are extraneous materials that shed doubt on it as a background text for the incident in John, it should be noted that an acceptable Hebrew scripture has yet to be found as background for these two passages, though of course many suggestions have been made.[11]

Edmunds' work retains its value because, even after seventy-five years, it remains the best sourcebook for displaying the parallel texts. Its weakness is that for the most part it leaves us on our own to decide if the parallel is thematic or a matter of historical influence.

Richard Garbe. Although he considered it to be proved that Buddhist stories in oral form influenced the apocryphal gospels and certain Christian legends from the second century onward, Richard Garbe was very skeptical of Buddhist influence on Christianity as early as the New Testament writings. In his early writings, he refused, on scholarly grounds, all claims of Buddhist influence on the canonical writings, but in his major work on the subject, which appeared in 1914 (in German),[12] he reversed his earlier position and admitted the strong possibility of Buddhist influence on the following four New Testament passages.

1) Garbe accepted the claim that the Lucan story of Simeon

was written under the influence of the Buddhist story of the sage Asita. He was convinced of this not only by the similar roles played by Simeon and Asita in prophesying the baby savior's future greatness, but by the fact that in both traditions this story follows an account of the angelic heralding of the savior's birth.

2) Garbe also believed the New Testament account of the temptation of Jesus by the devil owed some of its detail to the Buddhist account of the temptation of Gautama by Mara. Although Garbe realized that no single, extant Buddhist text parallels the Christian account fully, he was impressed by these similarities: a Satan figure personifying evil who appears and tempts the master to abandon his holy mission; the master's long fast; the idea that the master's career requires refusing worldly rule; the master's temptation to commit suicide; and the master's temptation to turn one substance into another.

3) The story of Peter's walking on the water is too similar to the prose portion of Jataka 190 (as discussed in the previous chapter) not to have been indebted to it, Garbe believed. Not only do both stories tell of a disciple who walks on water to his master, but also in both cases, the disciple started to sink when he lost his faith. The latter detail convinced Garbe. He notes that the Buddhist account, though written down much later than the Christian, antedates the New Testament and also walking on water by spiritual powers is a common theme in India and otherwise unknown in Jewish literature.

4) The Jataka story (no. 78) of Buddha's multiplication miracle is the fourth instance of Buddhist influence that Garbe accepts.

Having reversed his earlier position concerning Buddhist influence on the New Testament, Garbe somewhat reluctantly noted that if indeed these four passages were influenced, then it is probable that other passages, for which the similarities are less striking, may also have been influenced by Buddhist oral materials. He mentions the phrase "wheel of birth" in James

3:6 as an example of such a passage that appears to be Buddhist influenced.

Garbe was a more objective scholar than many other writers who have taken up this subject. He did not see his acceptance of some Buddhist influence on the New Testament as being of great significance to Christianity or Buddhism. But here and there, we detect his personal view that true faith in Jesus is not based upon miracles, and so Christianity should be the better off if it became known that such accounts as that of Peter's walking on the water and Jesus' feeding the multitudes were spurious additions to the true account of Jesus' life.

Garbe's scholarship is certainly impressive, and it has the advantage of being still in print.[13] He pays attention to the date of the Buddhist parallels and to Hebrew or Egyptian background passages that might lie behind an alleged Buddhist influence. He does not, however, make any use at all of New Testament criticism. For instance, one wonders if it is not important that two of the four passages he refers to occur in the fourteenth chapter of Matthew.

Dwight Goddard. A late arrival among the books on Buddhist influence, Dwight Goddard's *Was Jesus Influenced by Buddha,* appeared in 1927. He argued strongly for the hypothesis of Buddhist influence on the basis of the Buddhistic nature of Jesus' teaching and especially his life-style. He also accepted the alleged Essene connection, which had become one of the planks in the platform of the influence party. Goddard attempted to make a case that Jesus in fact indirectly followed the eightfold Buddhist path and taught the four noble truths. I do not find his arguments convincing, but they do demonstrate several points of life-style and teaching that Jesus had in common with Gautama.

S. Radhakrishnan. S. Radhakrishnan's comprehensive book, *Eastern Religions and Western Thought* (1939), contains a section in which he quickly reviews many of the parallels in the masters' lives and teachings that had been pointed out since the late nineteenth century. Having briefly presented them, in a

The Question of Borrowing

way that makes the parallels seem very striking, he raises the question of borrowing. He decides that the Buddhist texts are demonstrably older but mentions various ways of accounting for the parallel texts besides historical borrowing. For example, the spiritual aspirations of the Indians and the Jews (and others) were similar, so he sees it as natural that their respective moralists would express similar teachings. He points out that the form of the parable is admirably suited to religious instruction, so he is not surprised that both masters used parables, and so forth. In spite of such arguments, Radhakrishnan continues, there still remain similarities that seem to be more than coincidentally related. Radhakrishnan seems to accept the hypothesis of borrowing, but he softens his stand and concludes:

> Whether historically connected or not, they are the twin expressions of one great spiritual movement. The verbal parallels and ideal similarities reveal the impressive unity of religious aspiration. Buddha and Jesus are the earlier and later Hindu and Jewish representatives of the same upheaval of the human soul.[14]

Almost as an afterthought, Radhakrishnan introduces what I would consider a different position altogether—one that I will deal with later. He suggests that the Buddhist concepts and teachings may have infiltrated the circle of the evangelists, who mistook them for the words and deeds of the master.[15]

For reasons that are unclear, debate on the issue of influence waned during the thirties and then virtually ceased. Several learned Buddhologists, including Edward Thomas and Louis de la Valée Poussin, considered the topic and concluded that influence was not likely.[16] New Testament scholars were thus excused from seriously considering the matter, and, besides, no one had really argued the case for influence in a way that might engage New Testament studies. No historical or textual finds appeared that might have decided the issue once and for all, so the sun was allowed to set on the question.

In summary we may say that the work of the proponents of

the Buddhist influence hypothesis has not made a case that convinced a significant number of readers. Yet it must also be said that their arguments have been convincing enough to be seriously considered, despite the radical nature of the hypothesis. The arguments are at least strong enough to merit a careful reconsideration.

Two things are needed for such a reconsideration. The preliminary requirement is that a *review of the possibility of historical contact* be made, and that will be the undertaking of the remainder of this chapter. Then, in the last chapter, I shall present what I consider to be the most feasible *case for Buddhist influence upon the New Testament.* None of the previous authors have really tried to coordinate their accepted parallel texts with New Testament criticism, so I will have to break new ground. Once this is done, some New Testament scholars may wish to lay a foundation for an extension to New Testament studies and for the study of the historical Jesus. I will offer a glimpse of the new structure in the next chapter, but the picture will be only a preliminary sketch.

How Buddhism Could Have Influenced the New Testament

There are several routes that Buddhist sayings and stories might have taken to wend their way into the Christian Gospels, if in fact they did. They could have filtered into the Mediterranean environment, (1) before Jesus, (2) via Jesus, or (3) after Jesus. I will consider each of these three possibilities along with the arguments that have been advanced by their proponents.

Before Jesus. The most popular candidate for the route of influence in the minds of the earliest proponents of Buddhist influence was that of the "Essenic" milieu out of which Jesus himself was thought to have emerged. According to many scholars, from de Bunsen to Radhakrishnan, the wisdom of India must have somehow become incorporated into some of the sectarian Jewish communities in the era immediately preceding the birth of Jesus. Here is the way Radhakrishnan summarizes this position:

> Jesus, as we have seen, enlarges and transforms the Jewish conceptions in the light of His own personal experience. In this process He was helped considerably by His religious environment, which included Indian influences, as the tenets of the Essenes and the Book of Enoch show. In His teaching of the Kingdom of God, life eternal, ascetic emphasis, and even future life, He breaks away from the Jewish tradition and approximates to Hindu and Buddhist thought.[17]

There is indeed considerable evidence that Eastern, especially Iranian, thought played a part in the thought and life-style of some branches of Palestinean Judaism before the birth of Jesus. Now that the Dead Sea Scrolls have been scrutinized by scholars, it is no longer necessary to rely totally on early historians for an understanding of the Essenes—assuming that the members of the Dead Sea community were Essenes. When we had only this ancient testimony for the existence of this group of sectarian Jews during the time of Jesus, it seemed curious that no mention at all was made of the Essenes in the Gospels. And now that we know that a group was living on the edge of the Dead Sea, so close to the region where John baptized repentant Jews and Jesus himself, the biblical silence is even more puzzling.

Whether Jesus was in direct contact with the Essenes or not, it is relevant to note that the Essenes and also the important Pharisee party may well have been influenced by Iranian religious motifs. This is a complicated question that cannot be considered in detail here, but I will mention some of the points that have been argued. The dualistic language of light and darkness employed in some of the Dead Sea scrolls is so like Iranian thought that some amount of influence seems virtually certain. The texts speak of an angel of darkness who is evil and is diametrically opposed to the powers of goodness, led by the angel of light. The two spirits are in perpetual battle and will be until the final defeat of the evil one and the redemption of the world from his grip. Humans are caught up in this struggle, along with the whole of creation. These views appear to be borrowed from Iranian beliefs, especially as contained in the Zurvan sect of Zoroastrianism.[18]

The Iranian influence on Hebrew thought dates back to the later years of the Babylonian exile, when Babylon itself had come under Persian rule and as a consequence some Jews moved further East into Persian territory. One author[19] has pointed out that a passage in the book of Isaiah (66:17), which dates from the period of the exile, may well be speaking against a Persian ceremony. Other passages[20] in Isaiah seem to owe a debt to Persian literary forms, though again the prophet is clearly speaking from a Hebrew point of view.

A switch occurs in the centuries after the return from exile under the Persians, during which time some Hebrew literature begins to incorporate Iranian beliefs rather than speaking out against them. For example, the Persian view of the major world empires is reflected in the book of Daniel: "The author of Daniel simply adapted the Persian apocalypse to his own purposes, with some characteristic modifications."[21] And the late Hebrew work 4 Ezra incorporates an Iranian-style statement about the separation of families which will likely occur at the coming of the judgment day, which is especially interesting because Jesus sounds a similar warning.

Although there were Jewish precedents for describing the end days as troublesome ones, some of the descriptions of the end in Daniel are so characteristically Persian that the label "Persian apocalypticism" seems in order.[22]

Jacob Neusner has pointed out the similarities between "Rabbi and Magus in Third-century Sasanian Babylonia."[23] The primary function of the two in the eyes of the Iranian populace may have been that of healing, whether by medicine, bloodletting, or exorcism. Both were known to practice juggling, though their practice of astrology was surely much more important.[24] Neusner does not say that rabbis and magi were alike, but that the cultural milieu (which he calls Hellenism) had a common influence upon these two specialists from diverse traditions. He does not find evidence of this overlap in role between rabbi and magus before the third century, however, and if we take into consideration that such notions of merit have a long history in Iran and India, it seems more fair to speak of Iranian influence on the role of the rabbi than to speak only of a common "Hellenistic" milieu. In saying this, however, I do not mean to imply that Iranian religion was not itself influenced by Jewish and Hellenistic thought. On the contrary, I am impressed by the fact that most, perhaps all, major religions have grown and survived because of their willingness to borrow from and adapt to their purposes the ideas and practices of older and surrounding spiritualities.

With this thought in mind, that religions do borrow from one another, it is interesting to discover that Iranian notions of the judgment day have even found their way into the rabbinic commentary (Midrash) on the book of Isaiah. There it is said that at judgment "the wicked will be made to pass over the bridge of Gehinnom, which will then suddenly appear as narrow as a hair and they will fall into the abyss."[25] Winston comments, "This is certainly the Persian notion of the Chinvat bridge which appears wide and comfortable to the righteous, who are helped over it by a heavenly maiden, but for the ungodly it is so narrow and hair-sharp 'like a razor's edge,' that they fall helplessly into hell."[26] In this instance, the borrowing seems indisputable.

These Iranian-like images and beliefs in late Hebrew literature demonstrate that the Hebrews were influenced by Iranian thought in the period immediately preceding the time of Jesus. It has been suggested that the Jews who returned from Babylonia and Persia to settle in Jerusalem in the late sixth century before Christ brought with them some of the religious ideas that several generations of Jews had absorbed during their stay in or near Persia. This accounts for only part of the influence, however, because some of the late texts, such as the

Qumran Manual of Discipline, reflect ideas that had not yet developed in Persia itself until after the first groups of Jews returned from exile. In other words, *the influence of Iranian ideas must have been a continuing one* during the centuries leading up to and perhaps including the birth of Jesus.[27]

In fact the Zurvanite ideas involved are in some cases so late that Jacob Neusner is suspicious of the argument for Iranian influence on late Judaism on the grounds that the Iranian texts cannot be definitely dated before the Jewish texts which parallel them.[28] Neusner is right about the difficulty in assigning dates, but the content of the passages involved establishes them as more likely Iranian than Jewish in origin.

Such a line of argument establishes a fairly sound case for continuing influence from Iran, but it is much less certain what can be said about the possibility of Buddhist influence before the time of Jesus. Those who hold the "before Jesus" position can argue that just as the Jews, especially the sectarian ones, were open to Iranian influences in this period, so they may have been open to Buddhist ones as well. Furthermore, it can be argued that since Buddhism was rapidly spreading westward into areas formerly part of Persia, the same cultural connections that continued to bring Zoroastrian ideas into Palestine in the third and second centuries before Christ could have brought Buddhist ideas during the period immediately preceding Jesus. According to this model, we are asked to picture Jews from Parthia and other eastern fringes of the diaspora making the occasional pilgrimage to Jerusalem, spiritually armed with the latest religious doctrines, some of them Buddhist, of their home areas. The strength of this model lies in the fact that there is historical evidence that Jews did come from the eastern areas to Jerusalem and it could well be the case that they were becoming increasingly exposed to Buddhist missions in their homelands. This model does not ask us to imagine a Buddhist monk coming all the way to Palestine, there to preach to an audience that included the young Jesus. Rather we are to think only of a stream of increasingly

The Question of Borrowing

Buddhistic thought filtering into Eastern Judaism and from there westward into sectarian circles closer to Judaism.

The weakness of the model is that we do not yet have much evidence that such Buddhistic ideas, as opposed to Iranian ones, did filter into sectarian Judaism, yet we must allow for the possibility that such evidence remains undiscovered.

The idea that the Jerusalem and Galilean areas were exposed to Eastern influence before the time of Jesus is not nearly so far-fetched as it might seem initially. Two factors must be considered: Buddhism was expanding westward, and the East-West trade route traversed Palestine. This is not the place to review the history of the trade routes that connected India and northern China to the east with Egypt to the west; I must at least mention, however, that the famous "silk route" passed northward out of Egypt through Palestine, Syria, Mesopotamia (Iraq), Northern Persia (Iran), Bactria (Afghanistan), and on through Central Asia toward northern China.[29] This route had been followed for hundreds of years, with some changes and interruptions necessitated by warfare and climatic conditions. This land route across Asia included a major branch that extended south from Bactria down into the northwest part of the Indian subcontinent, passing through what is now Pakistan and from there connecting with other trade routes across India. There is some evidence that goods from India such as ink were being sold in Jerusalem, and certainly they were available in Egypt at the time of Jesus.[30]

In addition to this land route there was a sea route connecting eastern India and Egypt. By Jesus' time, the use of the monsoon winds in sailing had made this route an important one. Thus, sea trade with India became economically competitive with land trade, and as a result a considerable Roman presence was established in India, especially in the Andhra kingdom of East India. Roman coins have been found at several Indian sites. Certainly there were Indian merchants in Alexandria, and some evidence hints at the presence of a more permanent body of Indian immigrants in the city.[31]

Two Masters, One Message

These factors demonstrate only that there were commercial contacts on a regular basis between the East and the eastern parts of the Mediterranean, but other evidence points to the possibility of some contact with Buddhism as well. The story of this contact between Buddhism and the West begins with the missionary zeal of the Indian emperor Ashoka, who ruled in the third century B.C. In the previous century, Alexander the Great had conquered a portion of India; and his Greek-speaking successors held it briefly, until Ashoka's grandfather expelled the Greeks and set up a large Indian kingdom. Ashoka's father and Ashoka himself continued the wars of expansion until he had united nearly the whole of the subcontinent under one rule, a historic first. According to Buddhist histories Ashoka converted to Buddhism and its doctrine (Dharma) of nonviolence after winning the last and most bloody of his wars of expansion. Once converted, he became a zealous exponent of the new religion. He put up inscriptions urging people to follow the peaceful Dharma and also sent Buddhist missionaries to the Greek kingdoms. There is no evidence that such Buddhist missionaries ever reached as far west as Syria or Alexandria, Egypt, but there is evidence that Buddhists made serious contacts with the Greek-speaking people of the kingdom of Bactria. This kingdom was founded as an eastern outpost of the Alexandrian empire, and despite the fact that its populace was mainly Macedonian, it eventually became Buddhist in religion and figured as an important staging center for Buddhist missions eastward toward China and west at least as far as Parthia (Persia) and perhaps Syria. There were Buddhists among the Greek kings, the most famous of whom was Menander (known in Buddhism as Milinda). Ashoka himself had at least one of his rock edicts issued in both Aramaic and Greek—which happened to be the two main languages of Palestine in Jesus' time. A Greek coin has been found which features the inscription BODDO in Greek letters, and there is ample evidence that many of the caravan cities along the silk route were predominantly

The Question of Borrowing

Buddhist in the first Christian century and following. A caravan passing through Bactria (in the area of the modern town of Balkh, Afghanistan) would have passed by numerous colossal Buddha images carved in the cliffs.[32] These huge Buddha images still exist in Afghanistan, and they were accompanied with paintings illustrating Buddhist stories from the biographies and Jatakas such as the ones I have mentioned.

What school of Buddhism was responsible for the missionizing of the West? In the early second century B.C., perhaps, some Buddhists broke away from the Sthaviravada (Theravada) group and founded a new school of Buddhism named after their leader, Dharmagupta. It was probably this Dharmaguptaka school which was responsible for the spread of Buddhism beyond India in this early period. A. K. Warder writes, "This school made greater efforts than any other in spreading Buddhism outside India (to Iran, Central Asia and eventually China), with brilliant success."[33] Warder attempts to account for the Dharmaguptakas' phenomenal success in the spreading of Buddhism beyond India by maintaining that they modified Buddhist practice and doctrine in ways that would make it more appealing to the non-Indian populations. In any case, they spread Buddhism westward as far as Parthia and north far enough to intersect with the silk route, which makes this school or a related one the most likely candidate for the honor of succeeding on the western front. (It is significant that, of the four versions of the Dharmapada that survive, the one that seems closest to the New Testament is the Dharmapada in the Ghandari language; i.e., one that comes from the trade-route area northwest of the Indus River.)

As far as the sea route is concerned, Roman coins have been found in the Indian province of Andhra at the site of an ancient commercial city that contained a Buddhist temple. It is possible that Buddhism was spreading westward from India via the sea route and the land route. The sea route would have brought Buddhism into contact with early Christianity in Alexandria, while the land route passed through Syrian cities, some of which quickly became important Christian centers, and through Palestine itself. The proponents of the thesis that Buddhism had influenced Judaism before Jesus, could point to either route.

Via Jesus. A different line of argument involves describing a state of historical circumstances in which it could be said that Jesus himself came into contact with Buddhist teachings. The position that the influence was "via Jesus" himself has been especially popular among Indian scholars and, for different reasons, among Theosophists. I will consider the model imagined by the scholars first, setting aside the views of the visionaries for the moment.

An explanation that has been given from time to time is that Jesus himself traveled to India during his "lost years." Many imaginative attempts have been made to fill in the gap in the biography of Jesus between the incident in the Jerusalem temple at age twelve and the beginning of his public career at the time of his baptism by John at about age thirty. One such account is that Jesus spent some of those years traveling through India learning spiritual techniques from yogis, mystical lore from brahmins, and miraculous powers from fakirs. Some hold that Jesus also talked with Buddhist monks and Iranian magi. The difficulty with this account and other attempts to fill in the lost years of Jesus is very simply that there is no historical basis underlying them.

Perhaps the most famous attempt to write a gospel incorporating a trip to India is that of the Russian Nicolas Notovitch, who claimed to have received orally a translation of a "life of St. Issa" from a Buddhist source preserved in the Tibetan language.[34] According to Notovitch's Gospel, the one true God of the universe has assumed human form at various times for the sake of correcting human error and providing a path of salvation. Issa (Jesus) was born of poor parents near Jerusalem and at the age of thirteen was brought to India to learn from the Brahmins there. Upon his return to Palestine he preached to the Jews, saying that the true temple was within the

The Question of Borrowing

heart; the proper form of worship was purifying one's heart. Although he is said to have learned to exorcize and to heal while in India, there is little reference in Notovitch's book to his actually doing these things, as there is in the canonical gospels. The author used the format of a trip to the East as a means of accounting for the seemingly Eastern elements in the life and teachings of Jesus. This suggests the motivation for all the stories of Jesus' visit to India; such a trip would help explain many seemingly non-Jewish teachings and actions of Jesus.

Although there is no evidence for it, it remains a possibility that the young Jesus expanded his intellectual horizons considerably by traveling with a caravan east as far as Bactria or Parthia, for example, or south as far as Alexandria. In either direction, it could be argued, he might have come into contact with fragmentary accounts of the teaching of Gautama. If so, would we not have some mention of such a trip by Jesus? Perhaps not. Mohammed, the later prophet who lived among the Arabs in what is now Saudi Arabia, did travel with caravans, but these trips are seldom mentioned in the Quran.

Another possibility is that Jesus encountered Buddhist laymen or monks who were traveling through Galilee with a caravan.

A very different position is taken by those I shall call visionaries. From their point of view Jesus and Gautama, along with other masters, manifest similar actions and teachings because all true masters evolve from the same cosmic source. Some proponents would base such a view on a universalistic theology that holds that the one true God inspires masters from time to time in various places with an appropriate version of the "ageless wisdom."[35] This view is compatible with the theological tolerance of many Hindus, as expressed in the Vedic saying, "Men call upon God by many names, but wise men know that He is One."

The principle strength of the view that Buddhist influence came "via Jesus" is that the Buddhist parallels of the Sermon on the Mount and other similar sayings of Jesus have been ingeniously tailored to the Jewish listener. In no case are the borrowed Buddhist sayings used awkwardly or in a way unintelligible to Jewish hearers. The Greek is as good in the allegedly Buddhistic passages as elsewhere in the New Testament, for instance. This all points to a creative mind at work, and it has been argued that it seems most natural to assume that creative person to be Jesus rather than a later Jewish-Christian preacher. If this is true, the influence must have been either before Jesus or via Jesus—the two points of view blend, for in either case the influence has to come through Jesus himself.

The principle weakness of the argument that the influence came through Jesus himself is that it does not explain the Buddhistic nature of the stories told in Luke 2 about the birth and infancy of Jesus. Jesus never mentions these events himself, and Luke and Matthew do not claim to derive the infancy narratives from Jesus himself. This is to say, if we accept the usual scholarly opinion that the infancy narratives are a product of the early Christians and if we assume Buddhist influence upon these infancy narratives, then at least *part of the Buddhist influence came after Jesus.* This makes it tempting to see the whole of the borrowing as an activity of the early Christian church. In reaching out for additional information about the birth, infancy, and teachings of their master, early Christians reached too far and unknowingly incorporated into their records infancy narratives and groups of sayings modeled as much after an Eastern master as after their cherished Messiah.

Yet such a reconstruction of the alleged borrowing may be too hasty. How does one account for the Indian life-style that Jesus lived? For the Gospels record a life lived as a *homeless* (wandering) teacher and healer. The nature of his teaching is Jewish, and the nature of his healing seems folk-Jewish (at least it does not seem Indian); but as a homeless wandering teacher Jesus followed a pattern like that of Indian holy men. He went from village to village teaching (and healing), accepting meals from lay supporters, and attracted to himself a few "disciples," whom he trained to eventually continue his work. Where is the Hebrew prototype for this type of holy life? The prophets of an earlier day were settled men who were called to deliver a specific message, after which they returned to ordinary life. Even the newer movements within the Judaism of Jesus' century fail to provide us with models for Jesus' life-style. John the Baptist lived apart from society. The Essenes at Qumran had also withdrawn from society, but they certainly were not homeless.[36]

How are we to understand the life-style of Jesus then? Did he independently adopt an Indian-like approach, or had he heard about the way of Buddhist or Indian teachers? If so, it is strange that he never mentions India or Buddhism. On the other hand, many of the teachings of Jesus fall neatly into place if we keep in mind the Buddhist (Indian) distinction between the life-style of the "householder" and the "monk." The householder's role includes marriage, raising a family, and keeping intact family lineage and traditions. Men were expected to earn a living and women to care for the home. In addition, the devout householder was expected to give hospitality and other support to wandering teachers. The monk is to lead a life of celibacy and learning, sharing his knowledge of ethical and spiritual matters with lay people as he strives to lead an exemplary life.

The ethic of the two groups is quite different. The householder is obliged to support his parents, grandparents, and relatives and to procreate; whereas the monk is to give up all ties to home and family.

With this in mind, let us consider Jesus' harsh rebuke of two potential followers according to Matthew 8:18-22.

> Now when Jesus saw great crowds around him, he gave orders to go over to the other side. And a scribe came up and said to him, "Teacher, I will follow you wherever you go." And Jesus said to him, "Foxes have holes, and birds of the air have nests; but the Son of man has nowhere to lay his head." Another of the disciples said

to him, "Lord, let me first go and bury my father." But Jesus said to him, "Follow me, and leave the dead to bury their own dead." From an Indian point of view, Jesus is speaking to two men who have asked to be monks, full-time followers of the wandering master, who have not severed their ties to home and relatives. What would be obligatory for a householder—burying one's father—becomes unthinkable for a monk. What the householder takes for granted—the minimum security of having a roof over one's head—is not available to the wandering monk. There are many passages in Buddhism that make these points in various ways, including the Dharmapada verses on being content cited in chapter 2 and the following: "Let the wise man leave the way of darkness and follow the way of light. After going from his home to a homeless state, that retirement so hard to love" (PDh (R) 87).

Thus, the life-style and sayings of Jesus point to Buddhist influence upon the master himself, whereas the infancy narratives indicate that the influence may have been after Jesus. Perhaps we can solve this dilemma by considering further the case for influence after Jesus.

After Jesus. Actually there exists a surprising amount of evidence that Buddhism did in fact influence Christianity during the second and later centuries. Although my subject in this book involves the canonical sayings of Jesus and not the gospels of the second and third centuries, I will review the Buddhistic passages in these later gospels. For if it can be shown that Buddhism played a role in second- and third-century Christianity, the possibility that Buddhism also influenced Christianity in the first century is greatly enhanced.

We are aware that India and the West have influenced each other in the modern era; for example, to the English language itself, "India has contributed a considerable number of words. From its many languages, often very circuitously, we have taken over such terms as bandanna, . . . bungalow, calico, . . . jungle, loot, . . . pundit, . . . and sandal."[37] And the influence is not only verbal; for example, the word *pajama* and also the garment itself derive from India. Also, what we call Arabic numerals derive from India via Arabic. I suggest that just as in our time there are many ways in which Indian culture has influenced us, so in earlier centuries a similar process of unconscious borrowing occurred. From the beginning of British rule in India the influence has been more direct and intense, but the various avenues of trade and travel that have existed between India and the West since long before the time of Christ make it likely that some cultural interchange has occurred in nearly every century.

The most famous of all instances of Buddhist influence upon medieval Christianity involves the story of the Christian saints Barlaam and Josaphat (Latin: Joasaph).[38] These saints enjoyed considerable notoriety in the medieval Roman and Greek churches. According to the story, a prince was born as heir apparent to an Indian throne occupied by a tyrannical idolater who persecuted Christians. At his birth numerous prophets predicted his future greatness as a successor to the king, but one wise man said that the prince would achieve greatness but not as a ruler and that he would convert to Christianity. To shelter him and prevent his conversion, his father locked him in the palace. He eventually was allowed to leave temporarily and happened to see a crippled man, a blind man, and a senile man, and so learned of life's darker side.

Later a monk named Barlaam came to prince Josaphat in disguise and converted him to Christianity. Josaphat's father tried in vain to tempt him back to secular ways by magical spells, frightening spirits, and seductive women. The mature Josaphat shared the throne with his father for a few years, but abdicated after his father's death. He went in search of Barlaam, who was living as a hermit in the surrounding wilderness. En route he was again tempted, but he persevered for two years before finding his former teacher. The two lived as hermits until their deaths, when their bodies were taken back to the capital city and greatly honored. It should be added that alleged relics from these saints were later honored in Venice and elsewhere, and a church dedicated to St. Josaphat was built in Palermo.

Buddhist parallels (as told in chapter 1) to the Josaphat story are quite obvious. The storytellers framed Josaphat's early years with the story of the Buddha's birth, childhood, and departure. The Buddhistic parts of the story include the four sights (counting the coming of Barlaam as the fourth), the temptations, the period of struggle in the wilderness, and the eventual honoring of the relics of the holy man. It might seem that a real Indian Christian saint lies behind the Buddhistic legend, but the name Josaphat gives the lie to such a claim. For *Josaphat* has been convincingly shown to be a corruption of *Bodhisattva,* the title used for Gautama until the time of his enlightenment.[39] Also, some early Arabic versions of the story show no signs of "Christianization."[40]

The story of Josaphat provides us with an example of certain influence, so we can learn something about borrowing in the history of religions from it.

First, it is noteworthy that the story itself gives *no reference to the borrowing.* A student submitting such a tale to a professor without citing Buddhist references would be guilty of plagiarism, but religious stories are judged more by their audience appeal than by their footnotes, it would seem.

Second, we can see that when one religion borrows from another *judicious changes are made.* In this case the king's role is shifted from that of secular monarch to pagan tyrant. This change makes the story fit more neatly into the Judeo-Christian framework, where stories of idolatrous kings who persecute pious monotheists are par for the course. Also the major development in the life of the hero is changed from enlightenment to conversion, which brings the story into line with Christian experience.

Third, the *central ideas remain.* The plot of the story of Bodhisat shows through in the story of Josaphat. The old plot is wedded to the changes to make a new story, not a mere repetition of a foreign story.

Fourth, the new story even *serves a new moral.* In our case in point, the Buddhist moral conflict between the secular and the religious life has been to some extent subordinated to the moral conflict between Christianity and idolatry.

Finally, we can note that hints of the origin of the story survive in the *extraneous detail left unchanged.* In the Josaphat story these details include the names, the location of the story (in India), the idea of being confined to the palace to avoid knowing the ills of existence, the three (or four) sights, and the years of searching in the wilderness. In addition to these details, the storyteller has interspersed numerous parables, which should be carefully considered for evidences of Buddhist origins.

One manuscript of the Josaphat story, in Arabic, has appended to it three other, similar stories, which have recently been translated under the title *Three Unknown Buddhist Stories in an Arabic Version.*[41] The observations just made about the nature of borrowing are supported by these stories. Again there is no direct reference to the debt the author owes to Buddhism and, in one instance, to Judaism. Again the major story lines are intact, but some points have been altered or additional ones added in order to bring the stories into closer harmony with the spiritual values of the readers—who in this case are Muslems. Where Muslim users of the story share spiritual world views, little change is made. Where they do not, considerable distortion of the original story occurs. Also, various interpolations have been made that reflect Muslim piety. For example, when a king wishes to marry his daughter to the hero he says, "For if you would only see her and what amount of beauty and comeliness God has apportioned to her you would be delighted."[42] (In keeping with the original Buddhist plot, the handsome prince refuses the marriage proposal.) And again it is the untampered-with, extraneous detail that shows that the story is in fact not Arabic in origin. For example, a king abdicates when he discovers his first gray hair, a detail very often used in Buddhist stories but unknown elsewhere in Arabic stories.

Let us keep the general observations on borrowing in mind as I summarize a few other of the Christian tales that may incorporate Buddhist elements. One such story is the legend of the conversion of Eustace. According to the story the Roman emperor Trajan's foremost general, Placidus, was hunting and happened upon a herd of deer led by a particularly magnificent stag, which he followed deep into a forest. Then, the stag stopped, and he saw between its antlers a glowing (Christian) cross. At the same time he heard a voice saying, "Why do you persecute me?" The general returned home and converted to Christianity, along with his wife and two sons, and at baptism he was named Eustace.

Later, Eustace had a turn of ill fortune and in successive disasters lost his servants, his wife, and his two sons, which left him alone and destitute. Trajan summoned him to lead his forces against an uprising in the Eastern part of the empire. During this campaign he regained his family and returned to Rome in honor, but he and his family were martyred there as a result of their Christian faith, and later Eustace was recognized as a saint.

Richard Garbe[43] has put together a strong argument for Buddhist influence upon the Eustace legend. He believes the legend has three parts. The opening part, narrating the conversion of Eustace by a talking stag, derives from a Buddhist Jataka story about a magnificent stag.[44] The story line of the Jataka is different in some ways, but there are many similarities:

> The most important features are absolutely identical. The king Brahmadatta and Placidus are both passionately fond of hunting. In spite of this trait both are gentle in disposition but have not yet accepted the true doctrine. Both meet the Saviour of the world . . . in the form of a splendid stag—in the Jataka with silver-colored horns, in the Christian legend with the crucifix between the horns. In both stories the stag subjects himself to the danger of being slain

in order to point out . . . the way to salvation. Both . . . become converted through the stag and as a result attain heavenly bliss.[45]

In Garbe's scholarly opinion two similar stories can be accepted as historically connected if, in addition to having similarities in major points, they also have some "incidental features" in common. Such a feature is found in these stories, he argues, for in both cases the talking stag repeats his message to the king on successive days, for no apparent reason from the standpoint of plot development. Such repetition is common in Buddhist stories, which were intended for oral presentation, but there is no explicable reason for the repetition in the Christian story—except that its author was following the Buddhist version.

The second part of the Eustace legend does not come from the Jataka about the stag, but it has a parallel in the most popular of all Jatakas, the story of King Vishvantara. Both Vishvantara and Eustace fall from power and wealth and in the process lose even their wives and children. Both get everything back, of course—Hollywood endings are not new! The factor Garbe finds decisive for this Buddhist-Christian connection is another incidental detail that reflects the Indian origin. The village at which Eustace finds his family, while leading the Roman campaign, is said to be on the banks of the Hydaspes River, which is in India rather than in the Roman Empire. Under Trajan a great general, Marcius Turbo, was sent to crush a Jewish rebellion, but of course he never got as far east as the Hydaspes River. Alexander did get as far east as the Hydaspes, I might mention, and fought the battle of his life there against an Indian army employing elephants.[46]

The last part of the Eustace story tells how Eustace's family proved difficult for the new emperor, Hadrian, because of their strong faith. This account of the martyrdom seems modeled after Hebrew stories and evidences no debt to India.

Eustace, Josaphat, and Barlaam are not major saints, but there is evidence for Buddhist influence upon the story of a very well-known saint, Christopher.[47] The story of Christopher's later life and martyrdom follows the lines of so much of the Christian hagiography that we need not look elsewhere for its sources, but the story begins with the surprising description of the younger Christopher as a monstrous giant of a man with the head of a dog and the habits of a cannibal!

According to the story the powerful giant left the service of a king when he saw that the king feared the devil. He worked for the devil but again changed his allegiance—this time to Christianity—upon discerning that the devil feared the cross. Having become a Christian, he chose the path of good works, and taking advantage of his great height, he carried people across a river. One day the tall ferryman carried across a child, whose weight became enormous upon his shoulders as they crossed. Arriving on the other side, the child made it clear that he was the Christ and proceeded to baptize the giant in the water of the river. The giant was given the baptismal name Christopher, which means "Christ-bearer."

The suggestion is that the prototype for an animal-headed giant who carries the savior on his shoulders is converted by this spiritual passenger is to be found in the Buddhist Jataka story about Prince Sutasoma. According to the Buddhist story, Sutasoma allowed himself to be carried away on the shoulders of an animal-headed giant who made a habit of eating princes. By his honesty and righteousness Prince Sutasoma converted the monster to a life of genteel service.

The stories of Christopher and Sutasoma are by no means identical, but there are enough parallels to make the influence hypothesis acceptable. Garbe suggests that in this case the Christians may have learned of the story by means of a work of art at any one of the many Buddhist monuments that existed along the caravan routes. We have evidence that such Buddhist art did in fact picture an animal-headed giant carrying a man on his shoulders, as did the many representations of St. Christopher. One version of the Buddhist story says that the monster "lay in wait" at a pond and seized the prince as he emerged from a bath, which leads Garbe to speculate that the art object the Christians saw may have had the body of the monster partly submerged in water. This is possible, and would account for the role of the river crossing in the Christian legend, but no such example of Buddhist art has been discovered. As for the difference that the Christian story has a *child* Christ, whereas prince Sutasoma is an adult, Garbe explains that in the art work the prince appears rather small compared to the monster, which may account for the youthfulness of the Christ in Christian legend and art. In the Buddhist story the use of the term *prince* and the idea that he was carried on the shoulders might also account for the shift to a child savior, and the smallness of the Christ is in contrast to his great weight, as experienced by the giant.

In summary, there is good evidence for Buddhist influence upon part of the Christopher story, but it is not so strong as to convince all those who have investigated the issue. Assuming the story does owe a debt to Buddhism, we can learn from the Christopher legend that *sometimes the influence was pictorial.*

Could art have played a role in the transmission of the Eustace and Josaphat stories? Very possibly. For again the Buddhist stories involved are from the Jataka collection, which was the favorite subject of the early Buddhist decorative artists.[48]

The question of early Christians' exposure to Buddhist art raises the larger issue of the possible influence of Buddhist architecture and ritual upon early Christianity. Some researchers have become convinced that the Christian debt to Buddhism in these areas is considerable.

A lively debate has continued for years as to whether the Christian basilica is modeled after the Buddhist worship hall (Chaitya). There are many similarities, yet enough differences exist that the two styles of buildings could have evolved independently. There is no doubt that Greco-Roman architecture, especially stone work, influenced Buddhist art, so in this case intercultural *contact* is certain and some of the similarities may be accounted for by Christian influence upon Buddhism. Other similarities surely come from the common debt both traditions owe to Greco-Roman architecture. In spite of such observations, the debate about whether or not Christians borrowed the plan for their churches from the Buddhists will continue.

The argument for Buddhist and Iranian influence upon the decorative art of Christian temples, shrines, and other such structures is much stronger, however. R. A. Jairazbhoy has argued in detail the case of Eastern influence.[49] His research shows how widespread the cultural contacts and influences were, for they included artistic illustrations of hunting, hero stories, guardian animals, and war elephants. Only a few of these influences relate to Buddhism in particular, however.

Some aspects of the priest's clothing and especially the monk's garb have been considered to be Eastern influenced. For example, the word for the papal crown, *tiara,* may derive from a Persian word for a headdress. Garbe points out that the Buddhist version of this word, *civara,* refers to the monk's robe, but in this case, the Persian connection is probably the relevant one. Tonsure, the practice of cutting the monk's hair at his ordination, came into Christianity in the fourth or fifth century, perhaps from the similar Buddhist practice of shaving all hair from the head in preparation for ordination. It is possible that this custom was incorporated along with several other monastic practices from Eastern, especially Buddhist, monasticism. In Buddhism the shaving of the hair, according to a long Indian tradition, symbolizes the renunciation of worldly life and its pleasures, and the same symbolism fits the context of Christian monasticism.

For centuries before Jesus the members of Buddhist monastic communities assembled twice monthly for public confessions. In these sessions, which are still held, the abbot recites the many rules that the monks have vowed to keep, and if any monk has broken a rule, he is expected to confess his offense when the abbot pauses. If no one speaks, the abbot

The Question of Borrowing

assumes that no offense has been committed, and his recitation continues. This sounds very different from the current Roman Catholic ritual of confession, but there is some evidence that in earlier days that ritual was somewhat closer to the Buddhist one, which means that confession may have been accepted by Christians along with other monastic practices. There is little indication that Christianity borrowed its symbolic steeples, bells, and incense, yet the fact that these existed first in Buddhism merits a mention.

The possibility of Buddhist influence upon the rosary, on the other hand, is quite likely. The rosary came into Christian use quite late, and the word itself has been something of a mystery. Why would the string of prayer beads be called a "garland of roses" (or, "garden of roses")? A. Weber has proposed an intriguing explanation. The Buddhist term for prayer beads—which Indians have used for centuries—is *japamālā* ("prayer-garland"), which may have been mistaken for *japāmālā* ("rose-garland").[50]

Another suggestion is that the Indian origin for the Christian rosary is discernible in the arrangement of its beads in groups of twelve. The Christian practice of saying a decade of *Ave*, prefaced by a *Paternoster* and followed by a *Gloria Patri*, makes twelve prayers said on twelve beads. The twelvefold groupings in Indian prayer garlands probably were originally meant to correspond to the twelve zodiac signs.[51]

The Christian practice of venerating relics of the saints has a parallel in the Buddhist veneration of the relics of Gautama and subsequent saints. No firm evidence of borrowing exists in this case, but early Christian practices seem to have more in common with Indian counterparts than with those of Greece, Rome, or Egypt.

A more important topic for us, given the current debate within the Roman Catholic tradition about celibacy and the ordination of women priests, concerns the possible Buddhist influence upon the Christian practice of the celibacy of the priesthood. There has been a reappraisal of the role of celibacy in the early church recently,[52] which calls the primacy of the practice into question. This means that if Indian values concerning celibacy did influence Christianity,[53] the influence may not have taken place for a few centuries, until monasticism became important among Christians.

Besides the various Christian objects, stories, and practices that may have come into Christianity partly because of their previous use by Buddhists, there is the distinct possibility that Christian theology came under Buddhist influence. The place of intellectual exchange between East and West was Alexandria, Egypt, so it is not surprising that many of the Buddhistic points of theology come from the Greek theologians of Alexandria.

Some scholars have found considerable evidence that the impact of Indian ideas on Alexandrian intellectuals in the first Christian centuries was significant.[54] For example, the doctrine of reincarnation was widely discussed and was accepted in some of the philosophical schools of the day. Of course there was a precedent for the idea of transmigration in the thought of Plato, but Neoplatonism went well beyond Plato on this matter. One scholar, E. Seeberg, sees the influence of Indian ideas upon the Neoplatonic doctrine of the emanation of beings from the One and the division of men into two types according to their spiritual capabilities.[55]

It is thought that the person who connects Christian and non-Christian Neoplatonism with India is the Neoplatonic philosopher Ammonius Sakkas, who was the teacher of Plotinus, the founder of later (non-Christian) Neoplatonism, and also the teacher of the founder of Christian systematic theology, Origen of Alexandria.[56] The name Sakkas seems definitely Indian in origin, but it is not clear whether we should translate his name as Ammonius of Saker or Ammonius of the Sakka family. The Sakka family, by the way, is the same clan that Gautama belonged to, and the most common way of referring to Gautama in early Buddhism was by the word Sakya-muni, meaning "Sage (muni) of the Sakya clan." (Sakya is the Sanskrit spelling, but in other Indian dialects the word becomes Sakka.) This has led some scholars to wonder whether Ammonius Sakkas is not a reversed form of sakka-muni, but that lies within the realm of speculation. We can say that the name Sakkas points toward an Indian, perhaps Buddhist, influence upon Alexandrian thought in the third century A.D.

Tonsure, bells, basilicas, legends, teachers, confession, relic veneration, celibacy, rosaries, monasticism, incense—an impressive array of the components of early Christianity; so if several of these do in fact derive from Buddhism, the debt of Christians to Buddhists ought to be acknowledged. These borrowings, however, date from the third and later centuries, but could such borrowing have happened earlier? An affirmative answer is provided by the second-century writings of Christianity. Among the apocryphal accounts[57] of Jesus' life there are several incidents that seem almost certainly to derive ultimately from Buddhist biographies of Gautama. I will mention the most striking of these alleged cases of borrowing in brief.

At the birth of Jesus, Joseph saw the world and everything in it as if it had stopped, according to the "Gospel of James." Shepherds and sheep were motionless: even the heavens had stopped, for the stars and wind were still. The river did not flow, and the sheep that were in the act of drinking from it did not move. A similar cessation occurred at the time of the birth of Gautama, according to some accounts, such as the Lalitavistara account.

The young Jesus was venerated by dragons, according to the apocryphal Gospel of Matthew (called pseudo-Matthew), which parallels the veneration that the supernatural cobras (nagas) often give to Gautama in the Buddhist biographies. And we know from other sources that the nagas in Indian mythology were transformed into dragons as Buddhism spread to Southeast Asia and China.

Another apocryphal story (found in pseudo-Matthew) relates that Mary and Joseph (while living in Egypt) took the young Jesus into an Egyptian temple. To their astonishment all the images of the temple came to life and bowed down before Jesus. This story is reminiscent of the one told about the infant Gautama, according to which the images in a Hindu temple bowed down before him. This astonished parents and townspeople, of course, who had brought Gautama to the temple to perform the customary ritual of dedication. Both stories are intended to communicate to the hearer that the spiritual power of the child master is far greater than that of ordinary deities, and that even the deities worship him. It seems very likely that the Buddhist story served as prototype for the Christian version, which could hardly have been written by Christians of Jewish background.

Both young masters had an uncanny knowledge of the alphabet. According to the infancy Gospel of Thomas[58] the young Jesus was taken to a writing instructor, who was amazed to find that the child already knew the letters of the alphabet—a story that loses its punch in this age of Sesame Street. According to both the Buddhist and Christian accounts, the venerable old writing instructor fainted, falling down upon his face before the child. The irony in this would have been more apparent to ancient hearers, whether Buddhists or Christians, for the normal procedure would have been for the young pupil to bow down to the teacher.

In the Buddhist story the young Gautama then proceeded to astound the instructor by listing the sixty-four known alphabets (systems of writing), many of which the instructor himself did not know. In the Christian story the young Jesus shocked the instructor by not only reciting the alphabet but giving a mystical interpretation of each letter. These stories are so similar that most investigators have conceded that borrowing must surely have occurred, but which account is older? This story is not found in the earliest Buddhist biographies. It is found in the Lalitavistara and the biography that S. Beal translated as "The Romantic Legend of Sākya Buddha," neither one of which can be proven to be pre-Christian. However, the story fits nicely into the flow of the traditional Buddhist biographies, which say that the young Gautama excelled in knowldge of all the arts and skills (archery, horsemanship, etc.). On the other hand, the story occurs in only one Christian account and there is no hint at such an incident in the previous Christian gospels, unless it be thought that the incident of the twelve-year-old Jesus talking to the scribes in the temple is a sufficient precedent. Therefore I feel that the Christian story is modeled after the Buddhist one.

In addition to these apocryphal stories about Jesus, there are several apocryphal incidents concerning Mary that seem curiously Buddhist in tone. Most of these appear in the Gospel of James, which is primarily devoted to events that allegedly occurred prior to those covered by the canonical Gospels. The Gospel of James concerns itself especially with the story of the birth, infancy, and childhood of Mary; and much of the popular devotion to Mary is reflected in its pages.

At the age of six months, when she was first placed upon the ground, the infant Mary took seven steps toward her mother. Van den Bergh calls our attention to this incident as probably being modeled after the story of Gautama's taking seven steps (to the north) when first placed upon the ground after his birth. Taking seven ritual steps is a very old practice in India and is still today an important part of the wedding ceremony.

Several post-canonical Christian writings elaborate on the purity of Mary, sometimes in ways that resemble the Buddhist biographies praising Maya. According to the Gospel of pseudo-Matthew, Mary appeared luminous before she gave birth, and when she did give birth it was without impurity or pain. All three of these miracles are reported about Maya in the Buddhist biographies and even in the earlier, canonical account of the miracles surrounding the birth of Gautama.[59]

There is no hint at such miracles in the canonical Gospels, so it is possible that their existence in later Catholic piety owes something to Buddhist influence. A further hint at such influence may be provided by the depiction in Christian art of Mary with a transparent womb. Neumann[60] calls attention to the artwork on the left wing in a five-hundred-year-old church portal at Irrsdorf. Carved there is a pregnant Mary in whose womb one may see the radiant embryo. In the Buddhist accounts it is said that Maya could see the embryo she carried in her womb and that the embryo was luminous.

Another Buddhistic incident narrated about Mary is that a fruit tree once put down its branches miraculously. According to the Gospel of pseudo-Matthew, the young Jesus commanded a palm tree to bow down its branches so that his mother could pick its fruit to satisfy her hunger and thirst. This story seems to have enjoyed widespread popularity, for we have evidence of it in diverse places. For example, the Quran, which includes several references to the prophet Issa (Jesus), says that Jesus was born of a virgin under a withered date tree, and an English Christmas carol sings of the tree that bends down its branches to give cherries to Mary. The suggestion is that behind these Christian stories lies the Buddhist account of the tree that bent down its branch for Maya to hold while giving birth to Gautama. If so, the version in the Quran is closer to the Buddhist original in that it preserves the association with the act of giving birth.

In addition to these post-canonical stories about the lives of Jesus and Mary, there are a few sayings in early Christianity that may show Buddhist influence. For example, one post-canonical source attributes to Jesus the saying "Become passers-by." This presumably means "Sit loosely in the world" or as is said in Indian ethics, "Be detached." This interpretation is supported by a respected Muslim's version of the saying by Jesus: "Therefore live your life in it [the world] as men who are passing through, and not as men who have taken up their abode in it, and know that the root of all sins is the love of the world."[61] This is, of course, a saying that is so thoroughly in harmony with Buddha's teaching that one could preach a sermon on the text that would be well received among Buddhists. The first part of the saying—become passers-by—corresponds to the Buddhist ideal of becoming a wanderer, a homeless ascetic for the sake of spiritual knowledge. The second part about the root of all evil being the love of the world corresponds to the Buddhist teaching that craving, or attachment to the things of the world, is the root of evil. There are further amplifications of this saying that associate it with the notion that life is like a bridge—to be crossed but not clung to—which make the same point as the Buddhists do when they compare the doctrine (Dharma) to a raft to be used yet discarded when one reaches the other shore.

Another example of a Christian saying that has Buddhist precedent is the title "good physician" applied to Jesus. This title is common in the Buddhist texts[62] and fits in nicely with the idea that Gautama taught a "prescription" for spiritual health, for the Buddha's famous "four noble truths" are sometimes equated with the practice of a physician: "The truth of *suffering* is to be compared with a disease, the truth of the *origin* of suffering with the cause of the disease, the truth of the *extinction* of suffering with the cure of the disease, the truth of the *path* with the medicine."[63] Since Jesus healed many people and was understood as the *way*, "good physician" might be said to have evolved quite naturally out of the Christian understanding of Jesus; but there is at least the possibility that the title was appropriated from Buddhism.

I cannot resist mentioning one quite extraneous matter. The Christian debate about how many angels can sit on the head of a pin reminds me of a sermon of Gautama's in which he says that hundreds and thousands of angels came to listen to his discourse. They stood still in the air, above the ground, on no more space than would be taken by the point of a gimlet.[64]

Returning to the problem of dating the possible Buddhist influences, we can say that by the end of the third century there is little question that Buddhism was known in some detail in Alexandria and perhaps in Syria. The followers of Mani of Persia were spreading many Buddhist doctrines as part of their own religion. As for the second Christian century, the evidence is much less certain. Some of the apocryphal gospels with

Buddhistic passage *may* date from as early as the second century.

Besides the apocryphal gospels, the earliest Christian text that undoubtedly shows Buddhist influence may be the *Physiologus,* a zoological text perhaps of the second century, which includes descriptions of the charadrios bird,[65] the elephant,[66] and the unicorn that almost certainly derive from India.[67] The two most striking examples of Indian influence occur in the book's description of the unicorn and the elephant.

The evidence of Buddhist influence on the origin of the Christian unicorn motif is very convincing. First, the Latin term *unicorn* perfectly corresponds to the Pali word *ekasingam,* meaning "one-horn," which is used in Buddhist texts as the name of the rhinoceros. As for the context, the story of the princess and the unicorn told in the *Physiologus* certainly appears to be a Western reworking of a Buddhist story found in Jataka 526 and elsewhere in Indian literature. According to the Buddhist story, a kingdom was troubled by a severe drought, and it was thought that the only person with sufficient spiritual power[68] to force the rains to come again was a hermit sage named Rhinoceros, "One-horned." Since One-horned so thoroughly shunned city life, the king did not know how to convince him to come to the palace to work his magic. The problem was solved when the king's daughter voluntarily went into the forest, tamed the ascetic, and led him back to the palace, where he succeeded in bringing the much needed rains.

In the *Physiologus'* description of the unicorn it is explained that these animals can be caught (tamed) in only one way: a virgin girl must go into the forest and allow the trusting unicorn to place his head upon her lap, after which the tamed unicorn may be led back to the palace of the king. The Buddhist idea of the fertility that results from domesticating a unicorn/sage is missing from the description in the *Physiologus* but may be discerned readily in the unicorn tapestries of later Christian art, which picture a young lady and a tame unicorn surrounded by lush vegetation. The association of the unicorn with fertility

The Question of Borrowing

may antedate both Buddhism and Christianity. The fanciful animal is depicted in ancient Mesopotamiam art, so it is not argued that the whole of the unicorn symbolism comes from Buddhism. The suggestion instead is that the Buddhist story of the princess whose gentleness and purity tamed the unicorn came into Christianity as early as the second century, and this story was later illustrated by an ancient mythic animal representing fertility. As such it was a very popular subject in medieval Christian works of art.

Finally, I wish merely to mention the possibility that Buddhism influenced the various esoteric cults of the Hellenistic world referred to as "Gnosticism" by scholars. The Greek word *gnosis* means knowledge or wisdom, and the Gnostics were those who believed that they possessed a knowledge that enabled them to be counted among the "saved." These systems of salvation by knowledge remind us of the Hindu Upanishadic theme of salvation by the knowledge of the hidden relation of the inner self (atman) with the ultimate reality (Atman or Brahman). It is perhaps more relevant that the highest perfection according to much of Buddhist thought was the perfection of knowledge (prajñā). It is possible that Buddhism played a large role in the development of Hellenistic Gnosticism, in which case there would be further indication of Buddhist influence upon the Greek-speaking world in the first or second Christian century.

As one example of many parallels between Buddhist and Gnostic thought I would mention the fact that in both traditions the concept of wisdom—the key to salvation—was personified as a goddess. E. Conze lists these similarities between the Buddhist goddess Prajñāparamitā ("Perfection of Wisdom") and the Gnostic Sophia ("Wisdom"): Both are considered feminine, equated with the Law, thought to have always existed, said to be equivalent to the Deity, said to be the consort of the Deity, thought to be elusive, said to dispense the waters of knowledge to humans, destined to disappear in the last days, and so on.[69] These and the numerous other similarities between the two traditions cry out for some explanation of their historical connection, but the definitive answer still eludes us.

The evidence for influence upon Gnosticism, apocryphal Christian gospels, zoology texts, ecclesiological practices, and so on shows that Buddhism could and probably did play a role in the environs of the New Testament. Did it play a role in the shaping of the story of the infant Jesus or the record of his teachings?

IV
A CASE FOR BUDDHIST INFLUENCE

Q Is B: A Hypothesis

I have compared the stories that were told about the lives of the two masters and noted the similarities (chapter 1). I have also noted that many of the teachings of the two masters are curiously parallel (chapter 2). Having raised the question of borrowing, I reviewed a century of scholarship on the matter and considered the various suggestions that have been advanced to account for the historical connections between Buddhism and Christianity (chapter 3). Now it is time to build upon the foundations laid by previous scholars and propose a case for Buddhist influence upon the New Testament.

After presenting (in this chapter) a case I consider quite feasible, I shall discuss (in the conclusion) its implications for our knowledge of the historical Jesus.

In order to follow my line of reasoning, it will be necessary for the reader to understand what is meant in biblical studies by the term "Q." Thus, some introductory remarks on *the Q source*.

To understand the many discrepancies in the four Gospel accounts, it was necessary to determine which was written first, each writer's theological beliefs, sources of information each writer had, and when each account first appeared. The study of these and related questions, collectively known as biblical criticism, has led many scholars[1] to speculate that there was available to the early church a source of the sayings of Jesus that we do not now possess. In English this source may be referred to as the "Sayings Source" or a similar title, but it is much more common to refer to it as Q, which may derive from the first letter of the German word for source, *Quelle.*

Here in brief are the reasons for assuming the existence of Q. It is thought by most scholars that the Gospel ascribed to Mark is the oldest of the four accounts in the New Testament. Matthew follows Mark's account almost literally in many places, but greatly lengthens the story by the addition of many incidents. Of the additions made by Matthew, some are episodes reported only by Matthew and some are found in Luke as well. This raises the question of why Matthew and Luke report the same things at times while going their own way at others. The answer would appear to be that a collection (probably written) of the sayings of Jesus existed and was used by both authors but is now lost to us.

This means that the Q source may have consisted of those sayings (approximately two hundred verses) which Matthew and Luke have in common but which are not found in Mark. This is the definition of Q I will use in the first part of this chapter. Eventually I will have to consider the possibility that Q was a larger collection than just the joint Matthew-Luke sayings.

What is the theology of Q? Howard Kee and others have pointed out that most of the sayings of Q reflect the expectation that the end of the present world is at hand, that is, the expectation of the *eschaton.*[2]

Yet there may be conflicting understandings within the Q material. For example, do the sayings on treasures *in heaven* fit together with the expectation that the new era of God's rule is about to dawn *on earth?* Such a question opens the larger issue of whether Q itself is a composite source. Does it consist of mostly eschatological sayings plus some sayings on other themes such as nonviolence and contentedness? I will return to these questions after discussing the New Testament passages that reflect possible indebtedness to Buddhism.

I now wish to consider the evidence for my hypothesis that the Buddhistic passages may have come into the New

Testament tradition with the Q source. This approach is suggested by the fact that almost the whole of Luke's version of the Sermon on the Mount, a part of Q, has Buddhist parallels. Furthermore, several other of the parallel passages that I cited in chapter 2 on the message of Jesus come from the Q source. Let us consider whether Q is in part a Buddhist source—whether in part "Q is B."

The original order in the Q source was by topics, however loosely followed, and the consensus of scholarly opinion is that this order is best preserved by Luke. Therefore I will follow the order in Luke but will mention the corresponding texts in Matthew.

Temptation. It would seem that both Mark and Q had an account of the temptation of Jesus, for Matthew and Luke add the same details to the story as found in Mark (Luke 4:1-13; Matt. 4:1-11; cf. Mark 1:12-13). I have given Luke's account and some Buddhist parallels in chapter 1 (under "Quest and Temptation"), so here I will simply mention that the Q details are the ones that seem most like the Buddhist accounts—Matthew and Luke add that Jesus fasted and that he had a *conversation with the devil.* Satan's offer of the rule of the world is quite like Mara's tactic, and some of the proponents of the Buddhist influence theory have felt that the temptation to turn a stone into bread is inspired by the Buddhist story of Mara tempting Gautama to turn a mountain into gold (the story of Moses getting *manna* in the wilderness may account for the choice of words in this case). There is, however, no Buddhist precedent for the remaining temptation, to prove one's power by leaping from a great height.

Luke concludes the temptation story with the idea that Satan did not give up completely, but decided to wait until an opportune time. This same point is sometimes made in the Buddhist accounts: that Mara resolved to follow Gautama in hope of catching him in a thought of malice, lust, or cruelty.[3] Matthew instead chose to follow Mark's ending, saying that angels ministered to Jesus' needs. (Note that Matthew evidently did not use all of the Q material at his disposal.)

Thus it seems that Luke and Matthew expanded Mark's account of the period in the wilderness with materials from Q that were themselves based upon the Buddhist account of the conversation Mara had with Gautama while the young master lived as a fasting hermit.

Sermon on the Mount. The next material from Q that Luke incorporates is found in his version of the Sermon on the Mount (Luke 6:20-49; cf. Matt. chapters 5–7). Matthew and Luke group several sayings as a sermon, with a similar opening and closing, which suggests that such a grouping of sayings—beginning with the beatitudes and ending with the parable of the two houses—probably was to be found in the Q source. None of Luke's sermon is drawn from Mark, which further suggests that Luke may be reproducing the Q sermon rather closely.

I briefly mentioned in the "Be Content" section of chapter 2 that there was a Buddhist parallel to the saying about the blessedness of being poor, but with a somewhat different meaning. I will cite the four blessings from Luke opposite the four blessings from the Gandhari Dharmapada, changing the order of the Dharmapada verses to facilitate comparison.

Blessed be ye poor: for yours is the kingdom of God.	Happily shall I live, without property among possessors: Among possessing men, dwell without property.
Blessed are ye that hunger now: for ye shall be filled.	Happily shall I live, having no attachments, (We shall feast on joy like the angels.)[4]
Blessed are ye that weep now: for ye shall laugh.	
Blessed are ye, when men shall hate you, and when they shall	Happily shall I live, without anxious striving among strivers; Among striving men, dwell without striving. Happily shall I live, without hostility among the hostile;

separate you from their company, and shall reproach you, and cast out your name as evil, for the Son of man's sake. Rejoice ye in that day . . . Luke 6:20-23	Among hostile men, dwell without hostility. GDh 167, 169, 165, 166

The meaning of these four Buddhist verses on true blessedness is that the good disciple will find happiness in a life-style that avoids competition, hostility, and private possession. This is the essence of the life of a wandering holy man, as conceived in Ganges Spirituality. Do such sentiments lie behind the four "blessings" in Luke's account? A hint is found in the Greek word translated as "[you] poor," for the word chosen[5] can also be translated "beggars," who are quite different from peasants, however impoverished. That is, the Greek word used here may reflect a Buddhist background of wandering mendicants.

I conclude that there is a possibility of influence in the case of Luke's beatitudes, but the evidence for it is slight.[6]

Love your enemies. Luke continues his reporting of the Sermon on the Mount with the group of sayings that I discussed under the heading "Overcome Anger" in the second chapter. Luke's passage (6:27-36) has a strong parallel in the Dharmapada couplet that begins "conquer anger by non-anger" (GDh 280-81). The similarity in wording, meaning, and order of ideas, combined with the fact that both Luke and the Dharmapada repeat the ideas, make it quite conceivable that the Lucan passage on loving one's enemies represents an expansion of the Buddhist verses, with verses 31-34 on the golden rule and its application added to remind the readers that something more than worldly prudence is being demanded. The adaptation of the sayings to the monotheistic setting is apparent in the concluding appeal to become "sons of the Most High," as opposed to the Buddhist wording, "thou wilt attain the world of the gods."

Matthew gives a similar version of these sayings; so the

expansion of the Buddhist verses was already in the Q source—that is, unless Matthew used Luke as a source, a possibility I will raise in my concluding remarks.

Judge not. The sermon in Luke moves quickly from a statement that the disciple should not get angry with others to the point that the disciple should not judge the faults of others. In the earlier discussion of this passage (see "Do not be judgmental" pp. 66-67) I cited the close parallels (GDh 271-72). In both cases the opening injunction centers on a verb meaning "consider," "investigate," or "judge." The Dharmapada verb[7] would have been translated into Greek most appropriately by the very word that occurs *(krino)*.[8] And I could have translated GDh 271 as "Judge not . . ." rather than "Consider not. . . ." Also, the structures of the opening sentences have a similar tone because in both the Greek and the Indian versions the word for "do not" (judge) is placed at the beginning of the sentence for emphasis.

There are two obvious differences, however. One is that the biblical verse simply says "Judge not [others]" rather than specifying that the differences (faults) in others and what they did or did not do is the proper frame of reference for the injunction. This is not a significant difference because the omission does not alter the meaning at all and the following verses make the frame of reference quite clear. The other difference is that the Christian passage adds a new twist to the saying with the words "that you be not judged, and the measure you give will be the measure you get."

Luke's version adds further illustrations of the same ethical principle, which are not found in the two Buddhist verses. However, a Buddhist verse (Udanavarga 9.7, see p. 67) somewhat parallels Luke's simile of the cheating person as a blind man who may lead others with him into a pit—the "pit" is probably an allusion to hell in both the Buddhist and biblical texts.

There is no Buddhist parallel to Luke 6:40 concerning the disciple-teacher relationship, but verses 41 and 42, which return to the subject of not judging, make the same point as the second of the Buddhist pair of verses (272), which lends strong support to the possibility of influence. This is one case in which Matthew's version seems closer to the Buddhist.

If the Dharmapada verses against being judgmental did find their way into the Q source, then we can see that the sayings have been enlarged and perhaps a reference to God's judgment has been added.[9]

Luke's version of the sermon continues with some cleverly composed verses on the difference between persons with good minds (hearts) and those without. Matthew draws upon such verses as well, but he prefaces them with a saying about false prophets, which changes the meaning slightly from Luke's "make yourself a good producer" to Matthew's "watch out for bad leaders." Luke's closing verse ("Why do you call me 'Lord, Lord,' and not do what I tell you?") makes his meaning clear. People are admonished to follow the instructions of Jesus and become like trees that bear good fruit. This Lucan meaning is quite close to that of the Buddhist parallel I cited in the "Light the world" section (pp. 75-76). The Buddhist verse (DGh 258) expresses the negative instance, saying that "the fool who scorns the teaching of the worthy . . . persons . . . bears fruit to his own destruction like a thorn." The similarity in message combined with the similarity in the imagery of a thorn raises the possibility of some influence here.

This verse (GDh 258), like the Q passages, employs the thorn[10] as an example of a plant that is cut down because of its "fruit." In the GDh this verse occurs in the chapter on "teachers," which contains verses saying that the wise person pays close attention to the advice and example of wise teachers and scrupulously avoids that of fools. If we consider the previous verses in Luke on not condemning (good?) persons or blindly following fools, then we see that these Lucan sayings similarly encourage the disciples to distinguish good from bad teachers. Matthew's version emphasizes this meaning.

There are differences between the Lucan and the Buddhist sayings, of course. The Greek of Luke 6:43 is a beautifully constructed sentence that has no parallel in the Buddhist sources, but has something in common with Matt. 12:33. The Greek sentence consists of two fourteen-syllable clauses that are exactly parallel. Each clause consists of two-syllable words that occur in pairs and are connected by the verb, and the repetition and alliteration in the sentence serve to call attention to the opposition between good *(kalon)* and bad or rotten *(sapron)*.[11] So it is hard to imagine that this sentence is a translation from any other language, whether the Aramaic that Jesus is usually assumed to have used, or an Indian language. Yet how are we to account for the fact that Matthew does not have this sentence if it were part of the Q source or the original sermon? Perhaps Luke or someone he is dependent upon was responsible for putting the teaching into this striking form.

The other difference of note is that no parallel is given for the second part of the Lucan passage (6:45, cf. Matt. 12:35), about the good person bringing forth good from his good heart. Though there is no parallel to this in the GDh in the context of verse 258, other Dharmapada verses are worth mentioning:

> All that we are is the result of what we have thought: it is founded on our thoughts, it is made up of our thoughts. If a man speaks or acts with an evil thought, pain follows him, as the wheel follows the foot of the ox that draws the wagon.
>
> All that we are is the result of what we have thought: it is founded on our thoughts, it is made up of our thoughts. If a man speaks or acts with a pure thought, happiness follows him, like a shadow that never leaves him.
>
> (PDh (B) 1-2, cf. GDh 201-2)

Similarly we should take note of the fact that the Udanavarga pairs its version of the saying about the thorn with this verse:

> One must only speak what is right, and must not speak evilly; from wicked words comes evil, one ought consequently to use proper language. (Uv 8.8)

In summary, the imagery of the Lucan passage seems very Buddhistic, and this passage may be influenced by Indian thought. The Lucan simile of the thorn used to illustrate the teaching that one will die as a result of one's "evil fruit" has a strong parallel in the Dharmapada, although the mention of figs and grapes reflects the Palestinian milieu.[12]

The parable of the two houses. The sermon ends with the parable of the well built house that withstands the rains, in contrast to the poorly built house. In chapter 2, I gave a similar Buddhist saying in the section "Light the world" (pp. 79-80). Now that the question of influence is under consideration, let me compare the two passages in more detail.

Both the Buddhist and Q verses compare the good disciple to a well constructed house and the unwise one to a poorly constructed house. In both cases rain shows the weakness of a poor house. The Buddhist reference to having a "well guarded mind" and so being free of "evil desires"[13] makes a point similar to the biblical reference to the person who "hears my words and does them." The biblical passage does not mention the content of the teaching, as does the Buddhist, but the Buddhist call to be rid of "evil desires" is in keeping with the teaching that has preceded this passage in the Christian sermon.

The major difference in the simile of the two houses is that the biblical one refers to the foundation of a house, whereas the Buddhist one refers to the roof. The Indian passage presumably envisions a house that appears fine until the rainy season comes, and then leaks or is destroyed[14] by the onslaught of the torrential monsoon rains. The Palestinian passage is more explicit; the house stands until a flood wrecks it.[15]

Luke introduces the simile with a condemnation of those who call Jesus "Lord" but do not follow his teachings, and Matthew expands this by including other verses about hypocritical followers of Jesus. There is no Buddhist parallel to these introductory verses.

The parable of the two houses may be based upon the two Dharmapada verses (GDh 219-20). An explanation for the switch from a bad *roof* to a bad *foundation* is possible. The Indian house would have had mud walls and been roofed with thatch, so it would have been the case that the monsoon rains could destroy a poorly thatched house. The Palestinian house, on the other hand, would probably have had stone or brick walls with a flat roof made of wooden beams overlaid with clay.[16] If a Palestinian preacher had used the Indian version, his listeners would have had difficulty imagining a house destroyed merely by rains, which are not so severe in Palestine. (In another passage Luke may have changed the mud roof of Mark's account to a tile roof, to make the account more believable to his readers.)[17] The desire to make the account believable could account for the change to the image of a house being destroyed by rising river waters eroding the foundation. Matthew's version makes the destruction still more dramatic with the image of a torrent of "rivers" rushing at the house. Perhaps Matthew lived in an area where mountain gulleys *(wadis)* suddenly gushed with water during the rainy season. The expectation of a sudden, catastrophic end of the age, which is so evident in the Q material, may be reflected in the editorial changes made here. In the Buddhist context there was no need to have the house fall suddenly or completely, but in the hands of apocalyptic editors, the sudden collapse of the bad house may be intended to suggest what will happen to the evil persons at the apocalypse.

This completes the Sermon on the Mount according to Luke's version. There is a Dharmapada parallel to every portion of the sermon, with the exception of elaborations on the sayings and possibly the beatitudes.

Other Q sayings. Many of the passages from Q that have Buddhist parallels lie outside the Sermon on the Mount, especially outside Luke's version of it. I will continue my consideration of these texts by following Luke's order.

The Q version of the *transfiguration* (Luke 9:28-29; Matt. 17:1-2) of Jesus differs from the account in Mark, as I pointed out in chapter 1 (pp. 46-47). One of the Q additions is that the face as well as the garments of Jesus became radiant. Again I mention in passing that this addition could be explained by the influence upon the Q source of the Buddhist account of the glowing of Gautama's face. Luke adds that the disciples were sleepy, a detail that may owe something to the discussion of meditative trance that occurs in the Buddhist account just before Gautama's transformation.[18]

Another vague possibility is that the Q sayings on the necessity of *homelessness* (Luke 9:57-58; Matt. 8:18-19) may have been influenced by Buddhist verses such as those (PDh 91-92) cited in the first chapter (pp. 43-44). Dhammapada 91 points out that the true follower must leave home and give up the desire for security, and in the following verse on the same subject we have the reference to "birds in the air." The biblical reference to the birds having nests—not to mention the foxes having dens—is quite a different image from the reference to the miracle of flight in the Buddhist verse. Yet there may be some residue from the Buddhist verse in the Q expression "birds of the sky" or "birds of the heaven," for the Buddhist text has "birds in the air" or more precisely "in the ether," or heavens.

Following the sayings about the necessity of homelessness is Luke's account of the *missionary charge* to the seventy disciples (pp. 44-45.). Only Luke tells us that Jesus sent out seventy disciples, in addition to sending out twelve disciples on another occasion. Matthew uses many of the same words in his account of the sending of the twelve disciples, which means that the wording of the charge probably was found in Q. Perhaps the Q missionary charge made reference to the number of disciples as seventy, seventy-two,[19] or some such number, which Matthew ignored but Luke included in his Gospel.

If the Q version of the missionary charge was influenced by the Buddhist account, we could explain the existence in Luke of two missionary charges and some of the instructions that Jesus gave his disciples according to Matthew and Luke (as opposed to Mark). We would have to allow for a considerable amount of reworking of the instructions, however. The number of disciples had grown from sixty to seventy, the disciples are now to go in pairs rather than singly, and the imagery of the dust has been totally changed.

It may be worth mentioning that just as Luke continues with an account of the return of the seventy disciples, in which Jesus says "I saw Satan fall like lightning from heaven," so the Buddhist account of the sending of the sixty is followed by a dialogue between Gautama and the devil, in which Gautama proclaims:

> I am free from all the shackles,
> Whether human or divine;
> Freed from the strongest bonds, and you
> Are vanquished now, Exterminator.[20]

In the same passage Jesus says that he has given his disciples "authority to tread upon serpents and scorpions, and over all the power of the enemy; and nothing shall hurt you" (Luke 10:19). Following the Buddhist account of the sending of the disciples and the defeat of the devil is the story of the defeat of a terrible serpent that lives in the fire pit of an ascetic. The accounts are not really very parallel, but I wonder if the sequence in the Buddhist source had any influence upon the sequence in Q, which Luke follows here. The story of the master's walking on water closely follows in the Buddhist text, which might help explain how this portion of the story attracted the early Christians responsible for the Q source.

The Q saying about the *eye being the lamp of the body* (Luke 11:34-35; Matt. 6:22) has the Buddhist Dharmapada parallels that I quoted in chapter 2 under "Light of the world." The imagery is not quite the same, for the Buddhist verses do not equate the eye with a lamp, but the meaning is similar. The Buddhist verse (Uv 27.5) does equate the state of darkness with coveting worldly goods, which is also the meaning of the Q sayings. In this instance, the two Buddhist verses are not found together, which somewhat lessens the likelihood that they

A Case for Buddhist Influence

influenced the Q sayings. On the other hand, the possibility of Buddhist influence on the sayings about the "light of the body" is increased by the fact that Matthew locates them in his Sermon on the Mount, alongside other verses with Buddhist parallels.

Radhakrishnan[21] and other scholars have suggested that we compare the saying about the hypocrisy of the Pharisees with the following Dharmapada verse:

Now you Pharisees cleanse the outside of the cup and of the dish, but inside you are full of extortion and wickedness. Luke 11:39	What is the use of matted hair, O fool, what of the raiment of goat-skins? Thine inward nature is full of wickedness; the outside thou makest clean. PDh (R) 394[22]

If the Q saying was inspired by a Buddhist verse such as this, it has been adapted to a new setting. The Buddhist verse is directed against those who rely on ascetic practices, the biblical one against those who rely on ritual purity. In both cases, the masters insist that inward purity, havng a clean mind, is better by far.

The instructions to the disciples to *not be anxious* about their food, clothing, and shelter (Luke 12:22-31; Matt. 6:19-34) are like a page out of the Buddhist book, in meaning at least. Yet it is difficult to find exact equivalents among Buddhist sayings. I did offer a pair of verses (PDh 92-93) in conjunction with the saying "Be Content" in chapter 2 (p. 68), and we should consider the possibility of influence in this case as well. In the Buddhist verses the master is emphasizing that the real holy man, the good disciple, knows how to live and eat with moderation. In the Christian instructions the disciple is told not to be troubled about his personal security, but rather to have a faith that God will provide, as God does provide for the birds and other creatures. In each case, the implication is that the disciples should be content with a modest amount of material resources.

Luke's citation of the sayings against anxiety actually comes between two passages on the storing up of treasures in heaven rather than on earth. Under the topic "Store up heavenly treasures" in the second chapter (pp. 69-74), I gave these Lucan passages along with some very close Buddhist parallels. The story of the man who built bigger barns for his bumper crop, only to find that his life had been taken away from him before he laid up any *heavenly wealth* (Luke 12:15-21), has a parallel in three verses of the Dharmapada (Uv 1.20-22) that tell of a foolish man who rested content with the security of family and wealth, with no heavenly treasure to his credit. What good are worldly securities, the verses ask, when the lord of death comes to take one away? The meaning of the two passages is exactly the same, and the wording is similar—although there is no mention of barns in the Buddhist verses or of children in the Christian ones, and the biblical passage is in the form of a parable.[23]

After the story of the man with the barns, Luke cites the sayings against anxiety, which can be seen as painting the other side of the picture—the rich fool hoarded his wealth in order to feel secure, but the disciple is told not to worry about wealth or security but only about his esteem in the eyes of God. As a conclusion to the sayings against anxiety, Jesus instructs his disciples to sell all that they have in order to give to the poor, for by so doing they will have treasures in heaven (Luke 12:32-34.).

The Buddhist parallel (p. 97)[24] makes the same point, including the detail that the heavenly treasure is not subject to loss by theft and is worth our more careful attention. The "treasures in heaven" simile plays an important role in Buddhism, as may be discerned in the verses cited in chapter 2 on this subject, and lay Buddhist morality is centered upon the effort to "make merit," which brings blessings in this life and especially in the next.[25] This is the same meaning as in the Christian sources.

Besides the common theme, certain details occur in both stories as well. If we begin by comparing the Lucan versions with the Buddhist, we see that the structure is similar: (1) Perform acts of merit in order to accumulate riches in heaven; (2) for unlike earthly goods, heavenly treasure cannot decay of itself, nor can thieves or anyone else take it away from its rightful owner; (3) true contentment comes to the person who stores this kind of wealth.

Another consideration is that the conclusions to the Buddhist and Christian passages are phrased quite differently, although the meaning is similar. The differences seem less striking than the similarities in this case, so I accept this as a passage influenced by Buddhism.

Skipping to the sixteenth chapter of Luke, we find another saying that has a Buddhist parallel:

No servant can serve two masters; for either he will hate the one and love the other, or he will be devoted to the one and despise the other. You cannot serve God and mammon.	One is the road that leads to gain; another is the road that leads to *nirvāna*. Let the mendicant, the disciple of the Buddha, having learnt this, not seek the respect of men but strive after wisdom.[26]
Luke 16:13 (cf. Matt. 6:24)	PDh (R) 75 (cf. Uv 13.5)

Considering the Christian saying first, I am reminded of all the sermons I have heard in which the preacher struggled to apply this text to contemporary life—or rather to avoid applying it to contemporary life! For the saying quite clearly draws a heavy line between two life-styles, the one devoted to the physical and monetary security and the other devoted to the way toward God. The Buddhist saying is very nearly the same, except that it applies to those who have chosen to leave home—foregoing the pleasures and responsibilities of marriage and business—in order to devote themselves to a spiritual path. The verse that follows the one given above (Uv 13.6) makes this meaning very clear: "Retain no fondness for anything; deceive no man; give up any occupation; in [following] the law one must not be engaged in commerce."

I suggest that these Buddhist sayings influenced the Christian sayings in the Q source. If so, the original meaning was that the way of the wandering monk is different from and better than that of the lay person. But as we have the saying in Luke, it appears to apply both to the disciples who travel with Jesus and to other of his followers. Perhaps the whole of the Sermon on the Mount (this saying is part of Matthew's Sermon on the Mount) was meant to be instructions to Jesus' close disciples, who had given up all family relationships and personal security in order to help him. What they are to give up is *mammon,* a fairly obscure word in the Greek text, which is thought to mean both "wealth" and "property."[27] This is also the meaning of the Indian word used *(lābha),* meaning "gains" or "possessions" in this case. The disciple must not be anxious about such things, as Matthew's following verses spell out (Matt. 6:25-34).

Other Buddhistic texts in Luke. So far I have confined my discussion to texts from the Q source; that is, texts that occur in Matthew and Luke but not in Mark. However, there is no way of knowing whether the Q source contained some sayings that were used by Matthew or Luke but not by both. Perhaps Luke incorporated some of the sayings from Q that Matthew did not use, or vice versa. We know, for instance, that both Matthew and Luke chose not to use many sayings that were contained in Mark, even though they followed Mark's narrative framework. I will now consider several passages from Luke, and then in the next section from Matthew, that have Buddhist parallels but that are not found in any other of the Gospels. Whether these texts came from the Q source or from some other source known only to the evangelist who used them is a question that scholars have so far been unable to answer. Perhaps my arguments in this book will be of some help.

The most Buddhistic passages in the whole New Testament are the sixth chapter of Luke (his Sermon on the Mount) and the second chapter of Luke (his infancy narrative). The Sermon on the Mount sayings are found also in Matthew, but the infancy narrative of Luke is not. In the first chapter of this book I presented the many Buddhist parallels to the story of the birth

A Case for Buddhist Influence

and infancy of Jesus as told in the second chapter of Luke. Let me now reconsider these texts with the possibility of borrowing in mind.

Infancy narrative. Of the three chapters of prologue added by Luke at the beginning of the Marcan framework, there appear to be two cycles of stories—one about John and his relation to Jesus, and one about the birth and early life of Jesus. The stories about John have no parallels in Buddhist literature, but the birth narrative of Luke 2 is intriguingly parallel to the narrative told of Gautama the Buddha.

However one judges the parallels, the Lucan birth story is told with such an unmistakably Palestinian flavor that there are no grounds upon which to suggest that the Christian tradition appropriated the Buddhist tradition unaltered or in total. Rather, the Buddhist stories may have been used as a model for constructing the Lucan narrative or perhaps the Christian author(s) mistook the Buddhist legend for a Christian one and made numerous editorial improvements upon it to bring it into line with the geography of Palestine and the facts of Jesus' life as they were known.

Luke inserts in the story of John the account of the conception of Jesus (1:26-38). I have already discussed the Buddhist narratives that parallel this. In summary, the Buddhists related that Gautama was conceived nonsexually, by the direct descent of the savior-to-be (Bodhisattva) from a heaven through the side of Maya and into her womb. She was asleep at the time of conception and it occurred while she was observing a temporary vow of chastity. Once the divine embryo was within her, she refused sexual intercourse and, since she died shortly after giving birth, she never again indulged in sexual pleasures. The four archangels play a role in the conception, but not a sexual one. Mary, on the other hand is said to have been a virgin before her conception, which similarly occurred nonsexually. Luke, or some author he followed, may have included the reference to the nonsexual conception in his narrative because he was modeling it after a story that included such a claim.

Following the historical prologue, Luke's next verses in chapter 2 (6-7) quickly describe the birth of Jesus, as the firstborn of Mary, and adds the detail that the baby was placed in a manger. There is no evidence of Buddhist influence at this point, unless the story of Gautama's birth outdoors has played a role in the detail that there was no room in the inn.

Verses eight and following tell the story of the shepherds who were visited by the angels and who then came to venerate the infant master. This is the point in the narrative at which the Buddhist influence begins. In the first chapter (p. 24) I quoted the parallel story from one of the Buddhist biographies, which told that on the day of the birth of Gautama a certain holy man saw the angels (gods) sporting in the heavens, singing and shaking their garments (dancing?). When he asked them the reason for their gaiety, they explained, "In the city of Kapilavatthu, to king Suddhadana, a son is born. This boy will sit on the seat of Enlightenment and become a Buddha." I suggest that Luke's record is modeled after the Buddhist account: "For to you is born this day in the city of David a Savior, who is Christ the Lord." Luke adds to the story the message that the shepherds may find the baby in a manger, whereas the Buddhist account adds that the baby will be found in the king's palace and having the marks of a great person on him. The Christian account by no means slavishly follows the Buddhist, but rather (if at all) it models its story upon the narrative framework of the older, Buddhist account. Luke continues with the account of the arrival of the shepherds at the birthplace, which has no Buddhist equivalent.

There is a possibility that the source Luke followed was itself influenced by a Buddhist biography that included the detail that as the baby was born the workmen stopped in their fields, as did everything and everyone else. This could offer a partial explanation for the switch from one hermit to many shepherds.

The next incident in the Lucan account is the ceremony of

circumcision, which was performed on the eighth day after Jesus' birth. This parallels the naming ceremony, which was performed for Gautama on the fifth day. Both are routine ceremonies in their respective cultures and are reported routinely, so it does not afford us much evidence for or against the claim that the Christian story is modeled after the Buddhist one.

The purification of the baby at the temple in Jerusalem is the next event reported by Luke. After a prologue of his own authorship (verses 22-24), Luke relates the feature event of the episode, the encounter of the infant Jesus with the sage Simeon. The story of Simeon closely parallels the Buddhist story of Asita (p. 20), and most of the scholars who have written on the possibility of Buddhist influence have accepted this passage as being indebted to the Buddhist account. In both accounts an old sage recognizes the potential of the infant and prophesies his future greatness. Both sages allude to the fact that they will die before the child matures, a realization that causes the Indian sage to cry.

I believe that the convincing evidence for the hypothesis of Buddhist influence here is that both the first and the last part of the Asita story occur in the Christian account. We might dismiss the similar stories of Asita and Simeon as concidence, just as we might dismiss the similar stories of the angels rejoicing and speaking to Asita or the shepherds. But it is not merely coincidental that almost the whole of the Asita story appears in some form in the Lucan account. I suggest that the incident of Asita's conversation with the gods was the model after which the story of the shepherds in the fields was fashioned, and that the story of Asita in the palace is the model for the narrative about Simeon in the temple.[28]

Luke's story of the young Jesus ends with the famous account of his discussion with the teachers in the Jerusalem temple. Edmunds and other scholars have suggested that perhaps this incident reflects the story of Gautama's being honored by sages while his father was away plowing in a state ceremony. But the only two points of agreement between the two accounts are that both young masters are shown respect by "elders" and that the parent(s) is/are amazed to find the youth with a group of such elders gathered around him. Otherwise the stories are completely different, so much so that I do not imagine there was any influence in this case.

It would be better to suggest that the story of the young Gautama's being brought before the language teacher and amazing the old man with his learning might lie behind the Lucan story of Jesus in the temple. If so, we would have in Luke a mere hint of a Buddhist story that was later to come more fully into an apocryphal gospel, as discussed in the previous chapter. I consider the possibility of influence more likely in this case, although the stories are diverse.

Luke follows his infancy narrative with more about John the Baptist, which leads to the account of the baptism of Jesus—at which point his preface ends and he begins to follow Mark's framework, more or less. In addition to the Buddhistic points that both Matthew and Luke add to the temptation story as found in Mark, Luke also mentions that Satan followed Jesus, waiting for a weak moment, just as Mara is said to have followed Gautama. Luke's account continues with the Sermon on the Mount, with all its Buddhistic sayings, as I have already discussed.

The first passage after the Sermon on the Mount that has a possible Buddhist parallel is the story of the woman who wept at Jesus' feet and annointed his feet with oil (Luke 7:35-50). We should consider whether Luke revised the story (from Mark 14:3-9) of the woman who annointed Jesus' head with oil in order to combine this story with the one (from Q?) of a woman weeping at the master's feet. In light of the other Buddhistic passages in Luke, such a suggestion makes sense and would explain why Luke changed the story so drastically, whereas Matthew (26:6-13) chose to retell the story along the lines found in Mark.

Because in both accounts a woman addressed the master

A Case for Buddhist Influence

from a crowd, saying blessed is your mother, and because in each case the master affirmed that there is a higher happiness than that of having a fine son, Edmunds believed that the following incident reported in Luke may have been influenced by the Buddhist account:

As he said this, a woman in the crowd raised her voice and said to him, "Blessed is the womb that bore you, and the breasts that you sucked!" But he said, "Blessed rather are those who hear the word of God and keep it!"
 	
Luke 11:27-28
	At that time a kshatriya maiden named Kisā Gotamī had gone to the roof of the palace, and seeing the beauty and glory of the Bodhisatta, as he made a rightwise circuit round the city, she was filled with joy and delight, and breathed forth this solemn utterance:
	  Happy indeed is the mother,
	  Happy indeed is the father,
	  Happy indeed is the wife,
	  Who has such a husband.
	. . . Even to-day I must reject and renounce a household life, and go forth from the world to seek Nirvāna.
	Intro. to the Jatakas[29]

The stories are so different that I offer this only as a vague possibility suggested by Edmunds.

The next passage in Luke (and which is only found in Luke) with a Buddhist counterpart is the parable of the rich man with barns (Luke 12:13-21), which I have already discussed as being part of a group of sayings on treasures in heaven.

The account of the prodigal son is the next passage with a Buddhist parallel (pp. 83-84) that Luke alone includes. Since the hearts of the Buddhist and Christian parables are so similar, it is possible that one did influence the other. Actually in this instance there is a possibility that the influence flowed from the Christian to the Buddhist story since the Lotus Sutra dates from approximately the time of Jesus. However, in light of the evidence of Buddhist influence on Christianity, it would be wisest to say that the Buddhist story was the original. Based on this latter assumption, I will speculate on the way in which the Buddhist parable was reworked into the form we find in Luke.

In the New Testament story the starving son knows that he is coming to his father's house, whereas in the Buddhist story the father had moved and become rich, so his son did not know him. Perhaps the change was not deliberate, or perhaps the change to a father who had always been rich and who had a fixed residence made the analogy between God the Father and the rich father more apparent to the Jewish listener. Also, there is a change in the way the father reconciles the son to him. In the Buddhist story the father employs the son in a menial task and slowly increases his status and responsibilities as an employee until he eventually reveals to the son his true identity as a full heir. The Christian version has been altered so as to better fit the context in which God, through the actions of Jesus, offers *immediate* acceptance and sonship to lost members of the house of Israel.

Another significant change concerns the addition of the second son, which again helps the parable fit the Jewish situation in which other members of the Israelite household have been faithful servants of the Father all along and take offense at the amnesty and even high status given the returning apostates. There is also another explanation that we should consider. Matthew, and only Matthew, relates a parable about a householder who had two sons—one who refused to work but eventually did, while the other promised to work but broke his word. I suggest that Luke's parable of the prodigal son combines these two sources. That is, does the parable take from Buddhism the notion of the destitute son who returns and is received by the forgiving father, and take from another source (Jesus?) the saying about the two sons? This explanation makes sense, for it accounts for the source of Luke's long parable and at the same time explains the presence of the second son in the story. The remaining question is, why does Matthew give the shorter saying while Luke gives the long parable? Perhaps the shorter saying was a part of the Q source, with all its eschatological teachings, whereas Luke chooses to follow a more Buddhistic version.

In sharp contrast to the accounts of the death of Jesus in Mark and Matthew, Luke relates that one of the two robbers crucified with Jesus turned to Jesus in repentance and was converted on the spot. In the first chapter I compared this with Gautama's conversion of the bandit Finger-garland. The stories differ considerably, but Edmunds[30] was convinced that Luke had been influenced to include this episode in his account because he was aware that such an account was being told about the rival savior, Buddha. Edmunds' explanation is somewhat different from the one I have made, for I would say that there is a *possibility* that Luke combined two of his sources at this point by working in a "penitent thief" episode at the point in the Markan narrative where thieves are mentioned, namely, at the scene of the crucifixion. If so, Luke's editing in this instance would be consistent with what we have seen in his previous writing—he may be combining elements from a Buddhist source with the material from Mark and his other sources.

More Buddhistic passages from Matthew. I have dealt with those passages found in both Matthew and Luke (but not in Mark) which have Buddhist parallels, and I have considered the Buddhistic sayings found in Luke alone. Now I wish to mention some passages found in Matthew alone that have Buddhist counterparts.

Before considering the individual passages in Matthew I wish to mention that a few New Testament scholars have recently looked favorably upon the claim that Matthew may have been written by an early Christian in Syria or Mesopotamia, probably a Jewish Christian. If Syria is the place of origin for Matthew's Gospel, it would have come into existence in a part of the world that was certainly in touch with recent religious developments in Iran to the East and perhaps with developments slightly further East where Buddhism was becoming the dominant religion. Syria was located on the trade routes, and Antioch was not only a center of commerce but also became a key Christian city.

Recently, Robert E. Osborne has argued, from the point of view of New Testament formation history, that the Gospel of Matthew was written even farther to the East, in the upper Mesopotamian kingdom of Edessa (Urfa).[31] He believes that this city, with its large Jewish population and its location on the East-West trade route, was a very likely location for the writing of the First Gospel. He suggests that in this "provenance," influenced by Iranian and Indian theological motifs, Matthew wrote for his fellow Jews an account of Jesus suited to their understanding.

Osborne notes the following Iranian themes: Mithraic-like references to the sun and light, the virgin birth, Zoroastrian-like references to the magi and the star, the devil, furnace of fire, angels, the judgment of the dead after three days, and restoration of the dead.

The alleged Buddhist motifs mentioned by Osborne include the following: the use of the number six, reference to a person voluntarily plucking out his or her eye, the similarity of *yoga* and *zugon* (yoke), and the notion of treasures in heaven.[32] Osborne has put together an interesting case for Edessa as the homeland of Matthew's Gospel, but he has not taken into consideration the many other Buddhist passages found in Luke as well as Matthew. I will leave that question for the moment, in order to present the Buddhistic passages found in Matthew alone.

Matthew is the only evangelist to report that magi from the East visited the infant Jesus (Matt. 2:1-12). I compared this story with the Buddhist account of the role of the four archangels and the visit of Asita, in chapter 1. Here is the one place in the New Testament where the early Christians' awareness of things Eastern is obvious, for Matthew deliberately refers to them by their Persian name, magi. Osborne considers this good evidence for the origin of Matthew's Gospel among the Eastern Jews, and some of his supporting arguments have merit as well. In this case, there was Persian influence, not just *on* the story but *in* it, for the story says that some Persian astrologers discerned the event of the master's birth via the stars. There may be no Buddhist influence here, but the gifts that the sage Asita gives to the infant Gautama and the idea that Gautama was born under a certain constellation show that the Buddhist account is the *kind of story* which the Christian one is modeled after, if not the very story itself.

In the third chapter of Matthew (3:13-17) something new is added to the account of the baptism of Jesus, as compared to the version of Mark and Luke. John protests that he is not worthy to baptize Jesus, but Jesus insists, saying that it is proper. This episode has been compared with the protest Gautama offered against being taken to the temple to be dedicated to a god.

In the Buddhist accounts the young Gautama patiently explains to his stepmother that it is unnecessary for him to be taken to the temple according to custom because the gods have already praised him as god-above-gods, but he goes anyway to conform to propriety. These stories seem too diverse for us to suspect the Christians of borrowing, but one of the apocryphal gospels has an account that is closer to the Buddhist one. In the Gospel of the Hebrews,[33] it is said that the protest was made by Jesus, not by John. This change may be significant, for it could provide us with more evidence of Buddhist influence on later gospels, if not upon Matthew's.

I mentioned in chapter 2 (p. 63) the saying, which only Matthew gives, that the person who insults his brother will go to hell. The content of the verse is quite like the words Talmudic rabbis used in such discussion, so I doubt that there was direct Buddhist influence on the passage (Matt. 5:22), but there is a *possibility* of influence. Similarly, the idea that evil, adulterous *thoughts*—even if they are not acted upon—could send one to hell may owe something to Buddhist passages such as the one I quoted in chapter 2, under "Do not lust" (p. 65).

I would also point out that I compared the saying about not giving dogs what is holy, which only Matthew includes, with the Gandhari Dharmapada verse 273. This means that three verses from the GDh (271-73) may parallel Matthew 7:1-6. This group of sayings begins with "Judge not" and ends with the saying about dogs and swine. Luke gives the first part but not the last verse.

Matthew and Luke give quite different versions of the saying "enter by the narrow gate" (Matt. 7:13-14; Luke 13:23-34). They introduce the saying differently, and their interpretations vary as well. Luke's meaning is another version of "many are called but few are chosen," expressed with the familiar image of God as the householder who refuses to admit everybody into his household. Matthew on the other hand reports that Jesus contrasted the easy way of immorality with the difficult way of discipleship which leads to eternal life. Matthew's version differs so much from Luke's that one scholar concludes that Matthew has conflated sayings from two different sources: "We may, accordingly, assume that the evangelist has used both the Q saying much as it appears in Luke and also a saying about the Two Ways from another source."[34]

This raises the possibility that the passage in Matthew reflects a Buddhist saying such as the following:

> Life is easy to live for one who is shameless, who is of (the boldness of) a crow hero, for the mischief-maker, for the slanderer, for the impudent, and for the impure.
> But life is hard to live for one who has a sense of modesty, who always seeks for what is pure, who is disinterested, not impudent, who lives in purity; the man of insight.
>   PDh (R) 244-45 (cf. GDh 221-22; Uv 27.2-3)

But a better parallel, because it is more succinct, is the following: "Evil deeds, deeds which are harmful to oneself, are easy to do. What is beneficial and good, that is very difficult to do" (PDh (R) 163 [cf. GDh 264; Uv 28.16]).

A Case for Buddhist Influence

I find it most interesting that this verse, which parallels Matthew 7:13-14, is followed by the verse on thorns being destroyed because of their fruit, which parallels Matt. 7:15. Did Matthew find these two sayings together in the Q source? Were they together there because they were together in the Dharmapada?[35]

Matthew's saying about the wolf in sheep's clothing (7:15) has a vague Buddhist parallel, which I quoted in chapter 2 (p. 75). In this case we may also be dealing with two or more passages from different sources that have been combined.

The Matthean passage with the closest Buddhist parallel is undoubtedly the account of Peter's walking upon the water by faith (14:28-33). In the discussion of miracles (p. 93.) I gave the Buddhist and Matthean stories and pointed out that in both a disciple walks on the water by faith (or concentration), falters when the waves (or wind) pick up, and then regains his state of levitation by renewed concentration upon the master.

This is one of the parallels in which the influence could have gone either way, for the Buddhist story was probably put into writing later than Matthew's account, but on the other hand the motif of the (yogic) power to walk on water is a standard one in very early Buddhist doctrine. Thus, the evidence of literary dating might suggest that the Christian account is older, but the content would lead us to expect that this story originated in an Indian rather than a Christian milieu.

If the story did originate among the Buddhists and spread to Christianity, then we can see how Matthew operates as an editor. For Matthew follows Mark fairly closely in this section of his account until he comes to the story of Jesus walking on the water. At this point, quite logically, Matthew added the story he had heard or read concerning a disciple who had also managed to walk on the water. Since Matthew had a special interest in Peter, believing him to be the chief disciple, the "rock" *(Petros)* upon which the church had been built, it is understandable that he assumed that the unnamed disciple in the story was Peter. The other details of Matthew's version of the story were provided by the context into which he fitted it. The boat, the preaching, and the incident of faltering were easily incorporated by Matthew into the larger context as supplied by Mark's account.

One wonders why Luke did not use this story as well. This as yet unanswerable question reminds us that we have a very imprecise understanding of the nature of the Q material. Perhaps only part of the Buddhist stories and sayings had been included in the Q source, while other Buddhist stories such as this were circulating orally and not necessarily known to Luke.

Matthew's saying about the power to move mountains by faith (17:20) has a vague parallel in the Buddhist teaching that monks skilled in concentration could cleave a mountain. If it is the case that Matthew's editing involved the combining of sayings from various sources, perhaps he combined a saying about the power of faith, as in Luke's version, with the Buddhist teaching about cleaving a mountain. But this is admittedly speculative.

It has been suggested that Matthew's parable of the talents—about the three servants who fared quite differently when entrusted with money by their master, Matt. 25:14-30—was influenced by a somewhat similar story about three merchants found in the writings of the Jain religion of India. I do not think there are sufficient grounds for accepting Jain origin of this parable, however.

The saying, whoever serves the sick serves me, which has a close Buddhist parallel (p. 43), is found in Matthew only (25:40). The saying that the gospel will be preached throughout the world (Matt. 24:14) also has a Buddhist equivalent (see "How masters return" p. 46), but both are statements we would expect a master to make. More impressive is Matthew's addition to the record of Jesus' death, which incorporates the detail that the earth quaked, as it did at the death of Gautama (see under "How masters return").

These are the sayings with Buddhist parallels that are found in Matthew alone. Any of them could have been taken from the

Q source, as could any of the Buddhistic sayings that only Luke gives. So, if we allow all of these as Q materials, or materials from Q and similar sources that had been influenced by Q, we have amassed a considerable amount of *probable* evidence that in part Q is B.

Yet there are passages with Buddhist counterparts that do not come from Q, at least not as Q is usually understood. I must in fairness consider them before drawing my conclusions.

Evidence Against the Hypothesis

Mark. By anyone's definition of the Q source, the Gospel of Mark is separate from Q and does not draw upon it. This is not because Q was necessarily written after Mark, but because Mark is not supposed to have been acquainted with the Q source. Thus, it would be damaging to the hypothesis that in part Q is Buddhist if there are strong Buddhist parallels to Marcan texts.

I have argued that in several instances Matthew or Luke, or both, have combined some Buddhistic elements with a passage from Mark. Examples of this are the additions made to the account of Jesus' stay in the wilderness, the addition of Peter's walk to the story of Jesus walking on the water, and the addition of the detail that the earth shook at Jesus' death. Now I will consider some passages from Mark himself that have Buddhist parallels.

The first such passage in Mark is the *parable of the sower,* which many proponents of Buddhist influence have accepted as Buddhistic. In chapter 2 (pp. 80-82) I compared this parable (Mark 4:3-9) and its interpretation (4:13-20) with the Buddhist passage. The parables are similar but not so much so that a strong case for Buddhist influence can be constructed. It may be that we have in both cases parables taken from the same farming experience, and therefore they happen to be similar.

Mark follows the parable of the sower with another agricultural illustration, the *parable of the ripening crop* (4:26-29), which has the Buddhist parallel I quoted in the

Parables section (pp. 82-83). I consider this parable more likely to have been influenced by Buddhism than the parable of the sower, even though many previous writers have ignored it. Some New Testament scholars interpret the Marcan parable to be alluding to the miracle of a fast-growing crop, which would be quite unlike the Buddhist story, but it is also possible to interpret this as an illustration of the necessity for having the patience of a farmer—the meaning of the Buddhist story. The two illustrations are indeed similar, but again it is difficult to determine whether one influenced the other in instances such as this where the sayings deal with something so common as farming.

Many proponents of Buddhist influence upon the New Testament have cited the story of the *feeding of the five thousand* as one of their key proof-texts (pp. 88-89). My opinion is that even though the central miracles—the multiplication of bread—are quite similar, the many details of the stories themselves are diverse. I remain puzzled as to whether the Christian story was inspired by the Buddhist one. Richard Garbe, whose opinions on these matters are always carefully considered, accepts the "miracle of the loaves," as he calls it, as one of the four New Testament passages that he is confident were influenced by Buddhism. His argument is that in addition to the similar central miracle, the multiplication of the loaves of bread, there is in both stories the rather extraneous detail that some bread was left over. This is true, but there are also many points of divergence. For example, in the Buddhist story the disciple plays a major role, and the whole miracle is undertaken to convert a miserly couple. There is also the problem of determining which story is older, something that may never be decided in this case.[36]

I have argued that Matthew added from some Buddhist source the detail that the disciple Peter walked on the water on the occasion of Jesus' water-walking miracle. This approach fits the "Q is B" hypothesis quite nicely, but I must mention that some scholars have suggested that Mark's account (6:45-52) of

Jesus walking on the water has itself been influenced by Buddhism.

There are at least two Buddhist stories that may be offered as possible background to the New Testament account of Jesus walking on the water. Before taking them up I wish to mention that the belief that holy men can levitate, especially over water, was very common in ancient India but certainly was not among Hebrews, so a New Testament reference to walking on water raises the question of foreign influence.

One possible parallel to the story of Jesus walking on water comes from the incident in which Gautama rose up into the air and crossed the Ganges (p. 93). Comparing this story to that of Jesus, I note that there is no mention of the disciples nor of a wind in the Buddhist account, and no equivalent to the ferryman in the Christian account.

The other water-walking story told of Gautama comes later in the narrative, when he is attempting to convert the leader of fire-worshiping ascetics, Kassapa (p. 92). After several miracles failed to impress Kassapa sufficiently, Gautama miraculously walked on dry, dusty ground during the course of a raging flood. The ascetics and their leader were finally impressed and converted, and this incident was important to early Buddhists. Samuel Beal long ago noted that the event was depicted in the Buddhist art on the ornamental gate around the great stupa at Sanchi, India, and he imagines that it was similarly pictured elsewhere.[37] This art work brings the story closer to the Christian one, for in the artists' rendition there are disciples on the shore and there is a boat—which Gautama does enter according to the Buddhist story.

Neither of these stories is strikingly parallel, yet either of them, especially if transmitted partly through art, might have inspired the Marcan account, which Matthew and Luke follow. Matthew's addition comes from a different Buddhist story, I should mention, which discourages us from thinking of Matthew's account as a fuller version from the Buddhist source.

Some scholars have mentioned the following Buddhist saying about defilement as a parallel to the Marcan text:

Do you not see that whatever goes into a man from outside cannot defile him . . . ? . . . What comes out of a man is what defiles a man. For from within, out of the heart of man, come evil thoughts, fornication, theft, murder, adultery, coveting, wickedness, deceit, licentiousness, envy, slander, pride, foolishness. All these evil things come from within, and they defile a man. (Mark 6:18-23)	"Destroying life, killing, cutting, binding, stealing, speaking lies, fraud and deceptions, worthless reading, intercourse with another's wife—this is defilement, but not the eating of flesh." (Sutta-nipāta no. 241)[38]

These similar sayings are applied by the masters to somewhat different situations. The message of Jesus is apparently directed against those who were putting undue emphasis upon the necessity to wash before eating and to eat only certain foods appropriately prepared. Gautama, on the other hand, is speaking against the many Indians in his day who were convinced that strict vegetarianism was required in order to maintain spiritual purity. His own teaching on this issue was that the killing of an animal was wrong but not the eating of its meat—if it had already been killed for others and you were only eating leftovers. The similarities in the items that constitute real defilement can be explained as coincidental, owing to the similarities among all major ethical systems. Every society needs prohibitions against lying, cheating, stealing, and illicit sex, it would seem.

A Marcan text that has a closer Buddhist parallel is the illustration about the *widow's mite.* Mark (12:41-44) and Luke (21:1-4) report that once when Jesus was in the temple of Jerusalem he watched various persons putting their contributions into the temple offering box, and commented that the

A Case for Buddhist Influence

widow who had contributed two small copper coins had in fact made a bigger gift than had the rich men. The Buddhist story that parallels this tells of a poor woman who saw that men were holding a merit-making ceremony on a mountainside and went home to get the only thing she had of value, two small copper coins that she had found in the trash. She presented these as an offering, and the leader of the Buddhist monks interrupted the ceremony to commend the woman. He offered a verse that declared the greatness of her gift because it was given in total unselfishness. Such purity of mind had won her deliverance, the old priest announced. The woman then expressed her wish to be free of poverty, and the story concludes with a fulfillment narrative that says she was rescued from poverty on her way home by a king, who took her to be his chief wife!

The judgment as to borrowing in this case depends upon how one evaluates the similarity, "two copper coins." The Greek text says the widow put in two *lepta,* which is one *kodrantes.* The *lepta* was the smallest Greek copper coin, and the *kodrantes* was the Greek name for the smallest Roman copper coin.[39] This means that the widow put in two of the least valuable coins in circulation, as did the woman in the Buddhist story. In both stories the incident is observed and commented upon along the same lines, which may make borrowing a bit more likely.

Actually in this instance the borrowing, if any, may have been on the part of the Buddhists. The Buddhist text[40] was written later than the New Testament, and there is no evidence that the story antedates the author who included it, although it certainly may have. I see no way to decide which story is older and whether or not borrowing occurred.

John. Edgar Bruns, in *The Christian Buddhism of St. John,* argues more fully the hypothesis suggested in his earlier book, *The Art and Thought of John,* that "Johannine thought is structurally closer to that of Madhyamika Buddhism than it is to either the Judaic or Hellenistic categories of thought then current."[41]

Two Masters, One Message

Bruns does not locate the Buddhist elements solely in Gnostic texts, but writes that Buddhism and Gnosticism share the trait of believing in a secret revelation given only to advanced disciples. He writes, "We may then describe as characteristically Gnostic the presentation of a risen (and therefore glorified) Jesus who gives a special, higher, teaching to chosen disciples." The issue here is the means by which a sect manages to introduce new, yet authoritative, teachings into a religion. Bruns suggests that the Mahayana Buddhists had already faced and solved this problem by the first Christian century by saying that the savior appeared *after his earthly life* to a special group of advanced disciples, for the purpose of imparting to them esoteric teachings not parceled out during his regular teaching career. What distinguishes Buddhist and Gnostic handling of this issue, Bruns suggests, is that for the Buddhists, the new teaching given by the glorified master is for all to hear and not confined to an inner circle of initiates as in Gnosticism.

The author presents in capsule form several historical references that cumulatively make the point that there was in fact considerable contact, mostly in commercial trade, between India and the Mediterranean world in the early centuries of the Christian era. Bruns does not speculate as to exactly how John came to be acquainted with Mahayana Buddhist theology, but he does set the stage for the historical possibility of such an acquaintance. He argues that since it can be shown with fair certainty that some later members of the "School of John" (i.e., Basilides and some Gnostic Christians) were acquainted with Buddhist teachings, it is not impossible that John himself was at least somewhat acquainted with them.

The main Buddhist theological motif that Bruns finds in John is the idea that God is made present through love, which he believes parallels the Mahayanist teaching that Buddhahood (enlightenment) comes into existence upon the "perfection of wisdom." Bruns is struck by the contrast between this position and the Hebrew (and Christian) view of a God independent and above man: "It is unlikely that a first-century Christian would have constructed a theology so radically different from both Judaic and Hellenistic models unless he drew his inspiration from another cultural milieu, though the unique character of John's mind is not to be underestimated." (This line of argument is similar to that of Goddard.)

Buddhologists usually date the rise of Mahayana as roughly contemporary with the rise of Christianity, and if that is the case, Bruns' hypothesis asks us to believe that Buddhist ideas could have traversed westward very rapidly, which they may have. Even if it were chronologically possible for Madhyamika Buddhism to have swayed John, there is some question as to whether this particular school is the most likely source of influence. Also, is there in John any equivalent to "the thought of enlightenment" or to the Bodhisattva path—two central motifs in the early Mahayana scriptures? Is there in John any reference to the six perfections of Buddhist thought? And more importantly, why was a shift made from the Mahayana Buddhist emphasis on the perfection of wisdom to John's emphasis on perfection of love?

Yet, there are some Buddhist-like motifs that Bruns has identified. What he calls a horizontal theology is somewhat in harmony with the Buddhist understanding of mental cultivation or development of the mind toward perfection. But it is hard to imagine a Buddhist saying mental cultivation or the perfection of the six virtues brings *God* into presence. One can imagine a Buddhist influence on the terms "Way," "Truth," and "Light" much easier than on the notion of an inward "God." Bruns is no doubt aware of this and is arguing only that John's God brought into being in loving, is inspired by the Buddhist notion of Buddhahood brought into reality by compassion and wisdom. Such a claim should be considered alongside the other passages from John that I will discuss, and these include the passages on "the beloved disciple," which Bruns has discussed in a recent article.

The difficulty in dating also complicates the analysis of the

Buddhist and Christian stories about getting water from a lower-class woman at a well. I pointed out in the first chapter (pp. 40-41) that the act of asking a forbidden woman to draw water from a well is in both stories, but the two plots diverge after the opening incident. It remains a possibility that one story influenced the other, but it is not possible to say confidently which tradition may have done the borrowing.

The story of the woman at the well is the most likely case of Buddhist influence upon the Gospel of John, but other passages have been accepted as Buddhist influenced by various scholars, so I will now state their arguments briefly. One of the pioneers of the Buddhist-influence hypothesis, Rudolf Seydel, suggested that Jesus' puzzling statement to Nathaniel, "Before Philip called you, when you were under the fig tree, I saw you" (1:48), was a distortion of a Buddhist incident. Seydel suggested that by a slight alteration in the Greek manuscript the sentence would have the meaning, "When I was under the fig tree I saw you." This would bring the saying into line with the story that Gautama, after his enlightenment under the fig tree, saw with his magic vision the five ascetics at Benares and decided to go make them his first disciples. This is an interesting suggestion, but the evidence is slim and is tied to changing a word in the text.

A possible—but at best vague—parallel was pointed out by Edmunds between the disciples who turned back when they heard the hard sayings of Jesus (John 6:60-65) and the similar account concerning some of Gautama's would-be followers.[42] The stories are by no means identical, and the incident may well be authentic to both masters.

I feel that Edmunds' suggestion—that the saying "He who believes in me, as the scripture has said, 'Out of his heart shall flow living water,' " parallels Gautama's twin miracle—is not a good one (see note 21 of chapter 2). The other passage in John that Edmunds really believed was Buddhist influenced is the statement from the crowd that they have heard in the scripture that the Christ would remain forever. As I implied in my previous treatment of this parallel (see p. 102), I am not confident that this passage is Buddhist influenced, but rather accept the belief of many New Testament scholars that the text reflects a popular Jewish understanding of the messiah based upon some combination of scriptural ideas—as do many popular Christian beliefs about what is said in the New Testament.

I also do not accept the judgment of some that there is Buddhist influence upon the account of the disciples' question concerning who had sinned, the blind man himself or his parents.[43] The second part of the question is quite Jewish; there is no need to look eastward for the origin of the account, and Jesus' answer is not a Buddhist one at all.

Besides these specific texts for which Buddhist counterparts have been suggested, there is the possibility that Buddhist doctrines may have influenced the thought of John and thus may run throughout his Gospel. An example of this, in addition to those already mentioned from Edmunds' work, is the role that light plays in John's Gospel. It is true that light symbolism plays a role in nearly every religion, including Gnosticism and the thought of the Qumran community, so the mere identification of Jesus with light ("I am the light of the world") is not enough to demonstrate Buddhist influence. However, as Röhr[44] has discussed, Gautama did compare himself to a light. Some questioners asked which things light up the world, and Gautama in response listed four conventional things (sun, moon, day fire, night fire) and one unconventional thing: "But, of all things that shine, as best, light of a Buddha stands confessed."[45] Or more literally, "A Buddha shines best; this is an unexcelled light." But if there is a Buddhist influence on John's theology of light, it is a matter not of textual parallels but of ideological orientation.

Finally, an interesting suggestion has been made by Bruns to the effect that Gautama's personal attendant, Ananda, was the model used by the evangelist John in his presentation of *the disciple whom Jesus loved.*[46] His argument involves considerable critical detail about John's Gospel, but I will try to summarize his points simply. The author of the Fourth Gospel created the motif of the "disciple whom Jesus loved" and assigned him a very significant role. On the one hand, he testifies to the tradition of Jesus' sayings, and on the other he apparently is identical with the promised *paraklētos*, the "comforter" who will guide the community after Jesus' death. It is this beloved disciple who was with Jesus at his death—the eleven had fled—and who was the first disciple to recognize and testify to the resurrected Jesus. (The latter point depends upon some re-editing of the ending of John's Gospel.)

There is no parallel for the beloved disciple in the other Gospels or in Greek and Hebrew literature, Bruns notes. To find such a person one must turn to the Buddhist stories of Ananda, and these stories may have provided the theme that John suited to his purposes of establishing his own credulity as an evangelist (for his Gospel was quite different from the previous ones, and John probably saw himself as the *paraklētos*). Ananda was indeed Gautama's traveling companion throughout his mature years. Ananda was not enlightened at the time, but he did possess a remarkable memory, so after Gautama's death his disciples turned to Ananda to hear recited the numerous sermons of the master. According to tradition then, Ananda is the compiler of the "basket of teaching" (sutra) portion of the Buddhist canon. Bruns also finds it relevant that Ananda once stayed by Gautama's side even though the other disciples had left him during an attack upon the master's life.

There is one item of evidence that fascinates me although Bruns himself relegates it to a footnote, perhaps because of the possibly post-Christian date of the Buddhist text. In the Lotus Sutra, the same Mahayana text that contained the story of the "lost son," Ananda says, "I am the *parikāraka*," which means that he is the "one who is in attendance, in readiness."[47] From the context we know that this means that Ananda is at last ready for enlightenment, but given the function of Ananda as

A Case for Buddhist Influence

receiver and transmitter of the master's words, it is possible that a connection was seen by a translator (maybe someone other than John), between the Sanskrit *parikāraka* and the Greek word *paraklētos*. If the Lotus Sutra was presented (orally) in Greek and the word *paraklētos* used, it would be easy to imagine the evangelist John making the connection between Ananda and himself. According to this line of reasoning John would have adapted the notion of the beloved disciple who stuck by the master, remembered his teachings, and presented them after the departure of the master himself. Given the other hints at Buddhist influence in the Fourth Gospel, Bruns' argument remains a possibility.

Other New Testament parallels. In addition to the texts in Mark and John that have been considered Buddhist influenced by one scholar or another, there are two references in the letters of Peter that have piqued the curiosity of the proponents of Buddhist influence. In the first letter of Peter we read that after his death Jesus "went and preached to the spirits in prison" (3:19). This could possibly be an echo of Gautama's similar action, but the passage is so brief that it is impossible to judge.

The second letter of Peter contains this prophecy which sounds very Buddhistic:

The day of the Lord will come like a thief, and then the heavens will pass away with a loud noise, and the elements will be dissolved with fire, and the earth and the works that are upon it will be burned up.	Sirs, at the end of 100,000 years a new cycle will arise, this world will be destroyed, and the great ocean will dry up, this great earth and Sineru the king of mountains will burn and be destroyed. Sirs, practise friendliness, practise compassion, sympathy, and equanimity. Support your mother, support your father, honour the eldest in the family.
Since all these things are thus to be dissolved, what sort of persons ought you to be in lives of holiness and godliness, waiting for and hastening the coming of the day of God . . .	
II Pet. 3:10-12	Intro. to the Jataka[48]

Three points of comparison have been noted here.[49] Both passages address the reader as friend ("Sir") or "Beloved" (3:1). Both warn that the world is going to be destroyed by fire, which will burn up the earth and its mountains ("works" in Peter's account). And both urge the reader to do good works as a result of this warning. This passage in Peter's letter is complex enough and the parallels are such that I am inclined to accept the suggestion of Buddhist influence in this case. E. J. Thomas was not, I should mention, mostly because he was not convinced that the Buddhist passage is older. The dating question is insolvable (again), but the idea that the world will be destroyed by fire is very old in Buddhism, so I am willing to accept this passage as inspired either by Buddhist or Iranian notions of the end of the world.

I will end with a mention of the most Buddhist sounding phrase in the whole New Testament, "cycle of nature" or, literally, "wheel of birth" (James 3:6). This phrase has caused many translators headaches because it makes very little sense within the context of Hebrew thought. However, the same phrase, "wheel of becoming" (bhava-cakka) is a Buddhist metaphor for the key doctrine of rebirth. The best-known term for this among Western readers is *samsara (samsāra),* which refers to the constant wandering of the person from existence to existence, forming a chain or wheel of existence. Gautama once gave a sermon on the topic "All the world is on fire," and James writes in his letter that the tongue of man is on fire, setting the world on fire and being itself set on fire by hell. James' point—that man should curb his propensity to evil speech, slandering, and so forth—reads like a page from a Buddhist book. I can imagine that James, the champion of good works among the early Christians, could have employed the image of fire quite apart from Buddhist influence, but why would he use a Buddhist concept such as "wheel of birth" if not because his illustration owed something to Buddhism?

CONCLUSION

I have compared the lives of Gautama the Buddha and Jesus the Christ, with special attention to similarities. I concluded in chapter 1 that there were numerous similarities in the lives of the two masters, a point that has not been emphasized by most writers on comparative religion. Jesus and Gautama followed similar life-styles, traveling from village to village in order to teach, convert, and help people. Both gathered and trained a group of disciples and both laid the groundwork for a continuing spiritual reform that took the form of a new religion after their deaths. Their followers told similar stories about the birth and infancy of the two masters, and both masters came to be looked upon as more or less godlike.

The compatibility of the two masters' teaching, as discussed in the second chapter, is such that I suggested that they share a common message. The heart of that message is that the disciple should strive toward a pure mind, free from greed, anger, lust, and anxiety. They use metaphors from diverse cultural traditions, but the message is one. To help communicate this message, both masters worked miracles and taught in comparisons.

Because of the extent of the similarities, a few scholars have concluded that one master borrowed from the other. My review of these scholarly arguments in the third chapter noted that for the most part it has been thought that the Christians may have borrowed from the Buddhists, who were spreading their religion toward the West in the first Christian century. Thus, Christians may have been exposed to Buddhist art and literature, to modes of dress, and to wisdom sayings as well as monastic practices.

Finally, I assembled the evidence for Buddhist influence upon the New Testament. This consists of Buddhist parallels to New Testament passages, most of which are found in Matthew and, especially, Luke. With that in mind, I followed the order of Luke in the presentation so the reader could evaluate the hypothesis that part of the so-called Q source was itself heavily influenced by Buddhist sayings and comparisons. I have also presented the evidence against the Q is B hypothesis, which consists of sayings with Buddhist parallels from New Testament books other than Matthew and Luke. What remains is to evaluate the hypothesis that Q is B.

Appraisal of the Hypothesis

The argument for Buddhist influence is based upon the large number of New Testament passages with Buddhist parallels, not upon indisputable proof of any one of them. *The argument is one of probability* rather than certainty.

If there was Buddhist influence upon the New Testament, how did it come about? As a first attempt to explain this I have suggested that in part Q is Buddhist. Allow me to rehearse the evidence for that hypothesis and introduce three others.

1) Q is B. There are several indications that Luke and Matthew were drawing upon a source or sources that in addition to sayings about the end of the era also contained sayings that were in effect Jewish-Christian versions of Buddhist teachings. The Sermon on the Mount has the highest concentration of these Buddhistic sayings, but they are also found in quantity in later chapters of Luke and Matthew. Luke alone has the very Buddhistic account of the birth of Jesus, and the greater number of Buddhistic passages is in Luke. Here is a summary of them:

Conclusion

Luke	Topic	Buddhist Parallel (see list of abbreviations)	
2:8-14	Shepherds see angels	Intro. Jat. et al.	Asita sees angels
:21-24	Circumcision, naming	Intro. Jat. et al.	Naming ceremony
:25-35	Simeon prophecy	Intro. Jat. et al.	Asita prophecy
4:1-13	Temptation, fasting, and talk with Satan	Mv et al.	Gautama fasts and talks with Mara
Sermon on the Plain			
6:20-22	Beatitudes	GDh 165-68	True happiness
:27-36	No-anger	GDh 280-81	No anger
:37-38	Judge not	GDh 271-72	Consider not
:39	Blind fall into a pit	Uv 9.7	Cheaters fall into a pit
:43-45	Good and bad fruit	GDh 258	Fool bears bad fruit
:46-49	Badly and well built house	GDh 219-20	Well and badly roofed house
(End of Sermon on the Plain)			
7:36-38	Woman at Jesus' feet	Mv et al.	Woman at Gautama's feet
9:28-29	Face shines at transfiguration	Dialogues no.16	Gautama's skin glows
:57-62	Homelessness is good	PDh 91-2	Homelessness is good
10:1	Mission of seventy	Book of the Discipline	Mission of sixty
11:34	Eye is lamp	Uv 22.5 Uv 27.5	Wise man, with lamp Fool, in darkness
:37-39	Inward wickedness	GDh 2	Inward wickedness
12:16-21	Rich man with no treasure in heaven who dies suddenly	Uv 1.20-22	Rich fool with no treasure in heaven who must die
:22-31	No anxiety	PDh 92-23	The man who has no anxiety over food
:33	Treasure in heaven, safe from theft	Uv 10.11	Treasure in heaven, safe from theft
15:11-32	Parable of lost son	Lotus Sutra 4	Parable of lost son
16:13	Cannot serve God and money	Uv 13.5	Cannot pursue both Nirvana and wealth

Here are some generalizations that can be made about this list of Lucan texts with Buddhist parallels.

a) There are three sections of Luke that show a concentration of texts with Buddhist parallels. These sections and their parallels are as follows: Luke 2 and a Buddhist biography; Luke 6 and Dharmapada sayings on a pure mind; and Luke 12 (in part) and Dharmapada sayings on treasures in heaven.

b) The Buddhist verses used are employed in pairs. This is in keeping with their occurrence in the Dharmapada. They are separable, poetic units but in fact are often paired because of their content. The verses on the well roofed and badly roofed houses are good examples of this pairing. The Hebrew love of paired sayings may have made these Dharmapada verses more attractive to the early Jewish Christians.

c) Except for the Buddhist beatitudes, which are not strongly analogous anyway, the Buddhist parallels to Luke's Sermon on the Mount are mostly—if not all—from a few chapters that occur in the middle of the Gandhari Dharmapada, and these parallels occur in reverse order.

The list of texts from Matthew with Buddhist parallels is less helpful for assessing the possibility of Buddhist influence. However there is an interesting concentration of Buddhistic sayings in part of the Sermon on the Mount, and these sayings correspond fairly well with a group of sayings from the Dharmapada. I suggest then that we consider the possibility that the saying on God versus mammon goes with the sayings following it about anxiety, and that the whole passage was influenced by a group of Dharmapada sayings such as Udanavarga 13.5-10.

Matthew	Topic	Buddhist parallel	
6:24	God vs. mammon	13.5	Wealth vs. nirvana
6:25	Do not be anxious	13.6	Retain no fondness for anything
6:26	Look at the birds . . .	13.7	Look to your ultimate good; envy not others
6:27	Anxiety does not add	13.8	Put on this gown and seek alms
6:28	Consider the lilies		

Conclusion

6:29	Even Solomon was not as well clothed	13.9	Keep secluded
6:30	God clothes nature		
6:31	Do not be anxious about food and clothing	13.10	Be content with a little

Note also that a saying that occurs shortly after the above ones also has a parallel from the same source.

7:16	Know them by their fruits	13.1	Foolish man destroyed by honors (his fruit)

We could say that part of the Q source was heavily influenced by the Dharmapada and by the biography of the Buddha. If so, it can be seen that some version of the Dharmapada such as the Gandhari one and some version of the life of Buddha such as the one found in the Introduction to the Jatakas (Nidanakatha) lie behind the Q source. This is not to say that all of these Buddhist works were in Q, but that the framers of Q drew upon a knowledge of the two Buddhist sources, presumably without knowing their true origin. Luke may have had greater access to this Buddhistic material, or it may simply be the case that his editorial decision to make large insertions into the Marcan framework permitted him to use more of the Buddhistic material in Q than Matthew did.

Regarding the Sermon on the Mount in particular, it may be that in the beginning Luke drew from a source influenced by the Dharmapada (thus giving us a Buddhist sermon on the plain), then Matthew took Luke's small sermon and reshaped it as a rabbinical interpretation of the Deuteronomic demands of righteousness. This would explain how the Buddhist sayings got into such a Hebraic setting in Matthew and why Luke's sermon is almost totally Buddhistic, whereas Matthew's is not. Alternately, given the standard Q theorizing, one could say that Luke preserves the Q sermon (from a Buddhist source) but Matthew works with it in his own fashion.

2) Buddhist influence beyond Q. The few passages in Mark and John that show the possibility of Buddhist influence argue for this influence upon the New Testament, but they argue against the hypothesis that it came via some source (Q) known only to Matthew and Luke. The possible inclusion of Buddhist beliefs in the letters of James and Peter further suggests that the Buddhist presence among the early Christians was not confined to the Q source as it is usually understood. These other Buddhistic texts, if they are accepted as such, force a revision of the Q is B hypothesis along the following lines:

We could say that the Buddhistic sayings and the model for the biographic details about Jesus' youth come not so much from the Q collection of eschatological sayings as from some early Christian community. If so, we can imagine an area during the first Christian century (perhaps in Alexandria, in Syria, or even further east) that absorbed Buddhist materials in order to buttress the new religion—to make it more competitive in the world market, so to speak. This would explain why some Buddhist elements may have crept into the works of writers other than Luke and Matthew. It would also explain how, if influence upon John, Mark, and James occurred, more Buddhist works are involved than the Dharmapada and a biography.

According to the first hypothesis, we should imagine the Q community, wherever it was, absorbing two or three of the most popular Buddhist works and incorporating parts of them into records of Jesus. Then these records were utilized by Luke and Matthew and thereby gained widespread acceptance throughout the quickly expanding Christian world. According to the second explanation there would have been a fairly continuous flow of Buddhist sayings and biographic materials filtering into early Christian circles, to be in part rejected, in part put into Jewish-Christian dress and incorporated into the tradition. Perhaps each author found a few of the Buddhistic sayings helpful, while rejecting others. I can imagine Luke being pleased with the account of Jesus' nativity told upon a Buddhist framework, whereas John and Matthew were not—if they even knew the story. I can further imagine John accepting the sayings about light, the way, the beloved disciple, and the

Conclusion

Samaritan woman, but not others—just as he rejects so much of the material used by the other three writers.

The second hypothesis has the following advantages:
a) It allows for the diversity of Buddhist influence; the Dharmapada upon the Sermon on the Mount and other Q sayings; the biography of the Buddha upon Luke's infancy narrative and perhaps some other of Luke's private source; the Jataka stories upon a few of the parables; scattered discourse teachings upon scattered New Testament passages, and even later Buddhist texts upon later gospels, zoological texts, and hero legends.
b) It helps explain how the Buddhistic motifs were so readily accepted and transformed into Christian stories and illustrations, on the basis of continuing Buddhist influence.
c) It does not exclude the first hypothesis, for the earliest phase of the absorption of Buddhist sayings may have been the incorporation of part of the Dharmapada into Q.

Implications for the Historical Jesus

If some Buddhist sayings and concepts did find their way into early Christianity via one or more of the early Christian communities, what does that say about Jesus? It would mean that Jesus did not really teach the ethic of nonviolence, that there was no Simeon, no angels rejoicing at Jesus' birth, no dialogue with Satan, no Samaritan woman at the well, etc. If the Buddhistic parts of Luke and Matthew were subtracted, we would be left with a Jesus who was mainly a miracle worker and prophet of the End, not so much a teacher. The answer to this question cannot be determined with certainty, but we can consider the problem. Let me propose yet another hypothesis, in addition to the two considered above, which includes the historical Jesus.

3)   Influence through Jesus. Perhaps the Q sayings that have Buddhist parallels come from Jesus himself. That is, maybe Jesus had become exposed to Buddhist stories and teachings through some sectarian group within Judaism or through contact with travelers. Suppose further that Jesus chose a few of their sayings and images to incorporate into his own teaching, to illustrate his own theological position.

This hypothesis, that Jesus himself borrowed a bit from Buddhism, has several advantages as a way of explaining the parallels.

   a) It explains how the Buddhistic passages became mixed up with the eschatological sayings in Q: Jesus preached them all, more or less.
   b) It explains how the sayings became transformed so creatively; how Buddhist images have been skillfully used to make Jewish points.
   c) It allows for the diversity of Buddhist texts involved, if Jesus selected from among several teachings. This also explains why the Buddhist sayings are not exactly in order, but in groups, from various Buddhist sources.
   d) It explains why the Christian writers accepted these sayings—they would have been authentic to Jesus. (In saying this, I do not mean to imply that the record of Jesus' sayings was preserved impeccably.)
   e) It *may* explain the other Buddhistic terms, such as "wheel of birth" (James), and Buddhistic stories, such as Jesus' appearance before the writing teacher (Gospel of Thomas), if we imagine that the same Buddhist materials that Jesus drew upon were available for the other members of the movement as well.

There is one troublesome point about the third model. Although it accounts for the Buddhistic sayings ascribed *to* Jesus, it does not account for the Buddhistic stories *about* Jesus. I can imagine that Jesus preached the Sermon on the Mount (Luke 6) with images borrowed from Buddhism, but I cannot imagine the infancy narrative (Luke 2) going back to Jesus himself. How did the infancy narrative come to develop around a Buddhistic framework? Which early Christian modeled the stories of the shepherds and Simeon after that of

Asita? Luke does not even claim that Jesus himself told the story, and surely he did not, so who did?

To avoid this dilemma I will suggest a fourth and final hypothesis:

4) Continuing Buddhist influence. Jesus drew upon *Buddhist as well as Jewish concepts and images* in presenting his own teaching, which was not identical with traditional Judaism or with Buddhism. By this means the Buddhist ideal of nonviolence, the concept of treasures in heaven, the quest for a pure mind, and other Buddhist teachings came into the Christian tradition.

In his last years Jesus *lived a life like that of a Buddhist wandering teacher.* He traveled from village to village, performed miracles, taught in similes, and gathered about him a group of men dedicated to the same cause. That cause was mainly structured by the Jewish expectation of the coming era of rule by a direct representative of God, but the Buddhist life-style of Jesus (along with later developments) brought into the Christian tradition the distinction between the ordained, celibate, possessionless disciple (monk) and the ordinary lay person. The ethic for the two groups was different but complimentary.

The *Buddhist presence continued after Jesus' death* and influenced some of the early Christian communities to interpret the career of Jesus along the lines of a god-come-down (avatar). The doctrines of the preexistence of Jesus, the stories about his birth and infancy, and the belief in his return to heaven followed the Buddhist model. This avatar pattern was combined with other interpretations of Jesus derived from Jewish expectations: Messiah, Son of man, Descendant of David, and so forth. I suggest that the Buddhist avatar model helped Christianity transform the Jewish messiah concept into a savior figure that was understandable to the gentiles. Among the non-Jews of the West it enabled Christianity to compete successfully with the old Hellenistic and Roman cults as well as with the new Mithra religion of the Roman empire. Among the non-Jews of the East it enabled Christianity to supplant the old Iranian religions and ironically, to block the rapid westward expansion of Buddhism itself. Christianity was able in fact to win the Middle East and hold it for a few centuries, until Islam in turn spread northward from Arabia into the Christian East (as well as Christian North Africa). The stream of Buddhist influence upon Christianity was reduced to a trickle after Islam wedged itself between the Buddhist and Christian worlds, but even this small influence played a role in glorifying Christopher and other saints, in the adoption of the rosary and in the Christian practice (both in ancient and modern times) of meditation.

Later, the Christianity that Buddhism helped shape won Europe and reduced the old gods to angels and demons in the new scheme of things.

Meanwhile, Buddhism through the ages borrowed artistic techniques, organizational structures, and songs from the West, but that is another story.

NOTES

Chapter 1. Two Masters

1. As translated in Bhikku Nānamoli, *The Life of the Buddha* (Kandy: Buddhist Publication Society, 1972), p. 35; cf. *The Book of Kindred Sayings (Samyutta-Nikāya)*, trans. Mrs. Rhys Davids and F. L. Woodward (London: Pali Text Society, 1919–), v. 208.
2. *Dialogues of the Buddha (Dīha-Nikāya)*, trans. T. W. and C.A.F. Rhys Davids, *Sacred Books of the Buddhists*, vol. III (London: Pali Text Society, 1899; 3rd ed., 1951), ii. 4-41.
3. I shall use the term master, but the text uses *Bodhisattva*, a "being on the way toward enlightenment." The quoted passages are from the translations by T. W. Rhys Davids, who uses the shorter spelling, *Bodhisat*. The numbering system is not in the text, and my paraphrases abbreviate the original.
4. The Jain and many other Indian traditions also use the incarnation concept.
5. See the arguments in *Points of Controversy*, trans. S. Z. Aung and Mrs. Rhys Davids (London: Pali Text Society, 1915, 1969).
6. See *The Mahāvamsa: or the Great Chronicle of Ceylon*, trans. Wilhelm Geiger (London: Pali Text Society, 1964), pp. 51-54.
7. See Samuel Beal, *The Romantic Legend of Sākya Buddha* (London: Trubner & Co., 1875), pp. 36-41.
8. Cited from Edward J. Thomas, *The Life of Buddha as Legend and History* (London: Kegan Paul, Trench, Trubner & Co., 1927), p. 41.
9. One possible similarity pointed out by Edmunds is that in both stories the sage may approach the city by magical flight—for especially accomplished sages can fly. However, the reference to this magical flight, if it exists at all, is obscure in the Christian story. The most literal translation of the first part of verse 27 would be "And he came *on the air* to the temple. . . ." The word I have translated as "air" is *pneumati*, which can also mean "spirit," and when it is followed by the word "holy" it of course means "holy spirit" (as in verse 25). But here it is not qualified by "holy," although Christian interpreters have taken this to be implied. Presumably if Luke had meant this as a miraculous flight, he would have given it more emphasis. See Albert J. Edmunds and Masaharu Anesaki, *Buddhist and Christian*

Gospels, 4th ed. (Philadelphia: Innes and Sons, 1914), i.181-91. These words are spoken by Kassapa, not Gautama himself; but Gautama taught in this fashion as well.
10. Thomas, *Life of Buddha,* p. 42.
11. E.g., see Beal, *The Romantic Legend of Sākya Buddha,* pp. 42-43.
12. *Ibid.,* p. 58.
13. The biography of the Hindu god Krishna, who also comes to earth as an infant, tells that Krishna's family had to move to escape the vengeful wrath of King Kansa, who killed a baby whom he took to be Krishna. Some scholars have seen this story as strikingly close to that told in Matthew, while others believe the concidences are accidental.
14. *The Middle Length Sayings (Majjhima-Nikāya),* trans. I. B. Horner (London: Pali Text Society, 1954–), 1:300.
15. Cited from Nāṇamoli, *Life of the Buddha,* p. 21. Most translators have "plowing" rather than "working."
16. Nāṇamoli, *Life of the Buddha,* p. 21.
17. Cited, with omissions, from *ibid.,* pp. 19-20.
18. *The Mahāvastu,* J. J. Jones, trans., *Sacred Books of the Buddhists,* vol. XVII (London: Luzac and Company, 1952), ii.224.
19. The tempter himself mentions this prophecy. See Beal, *The Romantic Legend of Sākya Buddha,* p. 218.
20. *Ibid.,* p. 215.
21. *Ibid.,* p. 218.
22. *Kindred Sayings,* i.146.
23. For a detailed, scholarly comparison, see James W. Boyd, *Satan and Mara: Christian and Buddhist Symbols of Evil* (Leiden: E. J. Brill, 1975).
24. The last point is related only in Luke's account.
25. One of the best sources for Westerners to read on the tradition of the wandering holy man is Agehananda Bharati's *The Ocre Robe* (Seattle: University of Washington Press, 1962), an autobiography of an Austrian man who converted to Hinduism and became a traveling holy man.
26. Cited from Thomas, *Life of Buddha,* p. 242.
27. See Nāṇamoli, *Life of the Buddha,* p. 78; or *Book of the Discipline,* trans. I. B. Horner, *Sacred Books of the Buddhists* (London: Pali Text Society, 1938–), iv. 104.
28. I have altered Rockhill's translation at the end, where he has ". . . is a Sramana, a Brāhmana."
29. Cited from Edmunds, *Buddhist and Christian Gospels,* i.242. These words are spoken by Kassapa, not Gautama himself; but Gautama taught in this fashion as well.
30. *Ibid.,* ii.13.
31. Edmunds (ii.25) compares John 6:60-66 with Buddha's teaching titled "The Fire." See *The Book of the Gradual Sayings,* trans. E. M. Hare (London: Pali Text Society, 1965), iv.84-90.

32. Cited from Nāṇamoli, *Life of the Buddha*, p. 52.
33. Cited from Edmunds, *Buddhist and Christian Gospels*, ii.138.
34. Cited from *ibid.*, ii.124-25.
35. "The Heterodox Philosophical Systems," in Frederick H. Holck, ed., *Death and Eastern Thought: Understanding Death in Eastern Religions and Philosophies* (Nashville: Abingdon, 1974), p. 122.
36. As is the case with the other Buddhist passages cited in this section, this passage may be found in the Mahāparinibbāna Sutta, which is number sixteen of *Dialogues of the Buddha.*
37. Cited from Edmunds, *Buddhist and Christian Gospels*, ii.97.
38. E.g., see the discussion of the difficulty of identifying the source of this quote in Raymond E. Brown, *The Gospel according to John I-XII*, The Anchor Bible, vol. 19 (Garden City, N.Y.: Doubleday, 1966), p. 466. Prof. Brown accepts Van Unnik's suggestion of Psalm 89:36 as the most probable.
39. Cited from Edmunds, *Buddhist and Christian Gospels*, ii.170.
40. Cited from Thomas, *Life of Buddha*, p. 100.
41. See Samuel Beal, *Abstract of Four Lectures on Buddhist Literature in China* (London: Trubner & Co., 1882), p. 75.
42. William E. Phipps has recently investigated this assumption in his book, *The Sexuality of Jesus: Theological and Literary Perspectives* (New York: Harper & Row, 1973).
43. Later the image of the Buddha on the night of enlightenment replaced the stupa as the central cult object.
44. Wesak is the occasion of the birth and enlightenment of the Buddha as well as his death.
45. For more details on the Buddhist reinterpretation of Brahmanic sacrifice, see chapter 1 of my Columbia University dissertation, "The Concept and Practice of Doing Merit in Early Theravada Buddhism," 1970, available from University Microfilms.
46. Amore, "Heterodox Philosophical Systems," pp. 158-60.

Chapter 2. One Message

1. The translator left Brāhmana untranslated, but I have rendered it "holy man."
2. For a fuller discussion of the concept of death and afterlife in old India, see Frederick H. Holck, *Death and Eastern Thought* (Nashville: Abingdon, 1974), chapters 1-4.
3. Compare GDh 61; PDh 365-366.
4. See Amore, "Concept and Practice of Doing Merit in Early Theravada Buddhism" (dissertation, Columbia University, 1970), pp. 61-73.
5. Samuel Beal, trans., *Dhammapada with Accompanying Narratives* (Calcutta: Susil Gupta, 1952), p. 61.

6. E.g., see the parable of the avalanche, *The Book of Kindred Sayings,* trans. Mrs. Rhys Davids and F. L. Woodward (London: Pali Text society, 1919–), i.125-27.
7. Some scholars argue that the interpretation of the parable in the Gospels derives from the members of the early church rather than from Jesus himself. If so, the original point of the parable would probably have been that the disciples should persist in their teaching in spite of all manner of setbacks, just as the sower did, with eventual reward. This hypothetical interpretation concentrates upon the "sower," whereas the given interpretations center upon the "fields," as in the Buddhist text. See, e.g., Martin Dibelius, *From Tradition to Gospel* (New York: Scribner's, n.d. [German original, 1919]), p. 257.
8. H. Kern, trans., *Saddharm-Pundarīka: or The Lotus of the True Law* (New York: Dover Publications, 1963), chapter 4, verses 85, 91, and 97, pp. 88-90.
9. *Ibid,* pp. 108-9.
10. *Ibid.,* p. 99.
11. There is a problem in taking the second son as a representative of the scribes and pharisees, for the older son is far more noble—in spite of his jealousy—than the pharisees and scribes are said to have been in other of Jesus' parables. Perhaps it would be wiser to see the older son as the Jew who had remained faithful to God's Law but now was resenting Jesus' acceptance of those who had not.
12. *The Mahāvastu,* J. J. Jones, trans., *Sacred Books of the Buddhists,* vol. XVII (London: Luzac and Company, 1952), iii.116.
13. Beal, *Dhammapada with Accompanying Narratives,* p. 53.
14. *The Mahāvastu,* iii.244.
15. Commentary on Pali Jataka no. 78. See E. B. Cowell, ed., *The Jataka* (London: Pali Text Society, 1895, 1973), i.195-96.
16. See Beal, *The Romantic Legend of Sākya Buddha* (London: Trubner & Co., 1875), p. 255, for example.
17. *Ibid.,* pp. 240-41.
18. Cited from Nānamoli, *Life of the Buddha,* p. 148.
19. *Ibid.,* p. 59.
20. The story of the numerous miracles performed by Gautama to impress Kassapa and his disciples is found in the canon itself, in chapter 1 of the Mahāvagga *(Book of the Discipline,* IV).
21. *The Mahāvastu,* iii.115. Edmunds compared Gautama's twin miracle with John 7:38, which reads, "He who believes in me, as the scripture has said, 'Out of his heart shall flow rivers of living water.' " This passage from John has caused biblical scholars great difficulty, for it is not clear whether the living water is to flow from Jesus or from the believer, nor is it clear what scriptural passage is being referred to. (See Brown, *Gospel According to John I-XII,* Anchor Bible, vol. 19 [Garden City, N.Y.: Doubleday, 1966],

pp. 320-21.) What is interesting is that the Greek literally reads "from his belly," which Edmunds compared with "from his lower body" in the Buddhist account. The problems with this are obvious. There is no reference to flames or fire in the biblical account, and Jesus did not perform the feat of making water come from his "belly," he only talked about it. In the biblical context the miraculous waters are a sign of the coming of the spirit, perhaps, and a memory of the waters that Moses got from a rock during the Hebrews' stay in the wilderness. In the Buddhist account no symbolic meaning is attached to the waters that flow from the master.
22. Cited from Edward J. Thomas, *The Life of Buddha as Legend and History* (London: Kegan Paul, Trench, Trubner & Co., 1927), p. 241.

Chapter 3. The Question of Borrowing

1. Hilgenberg compared Buddhist and Christian texts as early as 1867, and Hardy's *Christianity and Buddhism Compared* appeared in 1874; but these pioneering works were necessarily based on very limited sources for the history and content of Buddhist texts.
2. Ernst de Bunsen, *The Angel-Messiah of Buddhists, Essenes and Christians* (London: Longmans, Green, and Company, 1880).
3. *Ibid.,* p. 165.
4. *Ibid.,* p. 167.
5. *Ibid.,* p. 171.
6. R. Seydel, *Das Evangelism von Jesu in seinen Verhältnissen zu Buddha* (Leipzig, 1882).
7. Van den Bergh van Eysinga wrote *Indische Einflusse auf evangelische Erzählungen;* Pfleiderer published *Christian Origins* (in English translation); and Schmiedel titled his work *Hauptprobleme der Leben-Jesu-Forschung.*
8. Edmunds and Anesaki, *Buddhist and Christian Gospels,* 4th ed. (Philadelphia: Innes and Sons, 1914), ii.71-72.
9. *Ibid.,* ii.38. See note 21 in chapter 2.
10. *Ibid.,* ii.97.
11. For some of these suggestions, see Brown, *Gospel According to John I-XII,* The Anchor Bible, vol. 19.
12. Richard Garbe, *Indien und das Christentum* (Tubingen, 1914).
13. Garbe, *India and Christendom: The Historical Connections Between Their Religions,* trans. Lydia Gillingham Robinson (La Salle, Ill.: Open Court Publishing Co., 1959).
14. S. Radhakrishnan, *Eastern Religions and Western Thought,* 2nd ed. (London: Oxford University Press, 1940), p. 186.
15. *Ibid.,* pp. 187-88. Radhakrishnan suspects that such blending of the two traditions might have happened in Alexandria, Egypt, for there is abundant historical evidence that there were Indians living there in the early centuries of the Christian era.

16. See Thomas, *Life of Buddha,* chapter 17, and L. de la Vallée Poussin's critique of the Edmunds book in *Review Biblique,* Paris, July, 1906, pp. 353-81.
17. Radhakrishnan, *Eastern Religions and Western Thought,* p. 176.
18. See, for an example of a scholar who argues this case, James H. Charlesworth, "A Critical Comparison of the Dualism in IQS III, 13–IV, 26 and the 'Dualism' contained in the Fourth Gospel," *New Testament Studies,* 1968–69, pp. 389-90.
19. David Winston, "The Iranian Component in the Bible, Apocrypha, and Qumran: A Review of the Evidence," *History of Religions,* Feb., 1966, pp. 183-216.
20. Isaiah chapters 40, 44, and 45. See the article by Winston just cited, p. 188, and Morton Smith, "II Isaiah and the Persians," *Journal of the American Oriental Society,* 1963, pp. 415-21.
21. Winston, "Iranian Component," p. 190.
22. *Ibid.,* p. 196. Winston points out that the belief that in the end days the lives of humans will grow shorter, as expressed in I Enoch (80:2), is characteristically Persian and is not found in older Jewish passages such as chapters 5 and 8 of Amos. Also we find in Jewish literature in this period the idea that in the end the mountains will be leveled and the sea will dry up, which is surely borrowed from Iranian notions. The book "II Enoch" is even more "saturated with Iranian material," Winston argues.
23. Neusner, in *History of Religions,* Nov., 1966, pp. 169-78.
24. Since I have written ("The Concept and Practice of Doing Merit," pp. 73-78) of the magical powers and spiritual qualities that come from meritorious practices, according to Indian Buddhist texts, I was interested to learn that a similar merit theory typified the thought of rabbi and presumably magus in this period. Miracles and unusual powers of protection were ascribed to rabbis of great merit.
25. Winston, "Iranian Component," p. 211.
26. *Ibid.,* pp. 211-12.
27. For the details of this chronological argument, see Winston, "Iranian Component."
28. Jacob Neusner, "Excursus," *History of Religions,* Nov., 1966, pp. 176-77.
29. A good source on the western cities along the land route is M. Rostovtzeff, *Caravan Cities,* trans. D. and T. Talbot Rice (New York: AMS Press, 1971; orig. ed. 1932).
30. E.g., see A. C. Bouquet, *Everyday Life in New Testament Times* (New York: Scribner's, 1953), pp. 118 ff.
31. J. Filliozat, *La doctrine brahamique à Rome au IIIe siècle* (Paris, 1956).
32. See Percy Brown, *Indian Architecture (Buddhist and Hindu),* 6th reprint (Bombay: D. B. Taraporevala Sons, 1971), p. 32.
33. A. K. Warder, *Indian Buddhism* (Delhi: Motilal Banarsidass, 1970), p. 289.

34. Nicholas Notovitch, *The Unknown Life of Christ,* trans. Alexina Loranger (Chicago: Rand, McNally & Co., 1894).
35. A somewhat different twist was given the universalist view by the movement known as Theosophy. This group sought to transcend the differences between Hinduism and Christianity, and this may have in part motivated their belief that the great prophets have themselves been mystically instructed by transcendental masters. This belief accounts for the similarities in Buddhist and Christian teachings, but it is not subject to historical proof.
36. E.g., see the article "Essenes" in *The Interpreter's Dictionary of the Bible* (Nashville: Abingdon, 1962).
37. Stuart Robertson and Frederic G. Cassidy, *The Development of Modern English,* 2nd ed. (Englewood Cliffs, N.J.: Prentice-Hall, 1954), p. 168.
38. Based on the idea that John of Damascus had told their story, they were accepted as saints, although there is some dispute whether it is correct to say they were canonized. The Roman Church celebrated their sainthood on November 27, and the Greek Orthodox Church dedicated August 26 to St. Josaphat. Their story was told far and wide among Christians, and we have extant Ethiopian, Greek, Arabic, and other versions of the story. For a summary of the story of Barlaam and Josaphat and its possible Buddhist connections, see, e.g., Garbe, *India and Christendom,* pp. 80-84; and "Barlaam and Josaphat" in *Encyclopaedia Britannica,* 1957 edition. For the full story, see, e.g., Sir E. A. Wallis Budge, *Barlam and Yesasef* (Cambridge: The University Press, 1923) or D. M. Lang, trans., *The Balavariani: A Tale from the Christian East* (Berkeley: University of California Press, 1966).
39. The arguments for the Indian reconstructions of the names were done long ago by E. Kuhn. The argument is complex, but the difference in length in the two words is easily understood when we realize that Indians often drop the last syllable of words, if the vowel is a short *a.* E.g., *rāja* (king) becomes *rāj* in Hindi, *Bodhisattva* becomes *Bodhisat,* etc. Of course the same thing has happened in English pronunciation of the Aryan language; consider the way the endings have disappeared from modern English as opposed to German or middle English, e.g., Chaucer's Prologue to *The Canterbury Tales,* where he writes "Whan that Aprille with his shoures soote. The droghte of Marche hath percéd to the roote."
40. S. M. Stern and Sofie Walzer, *Three Unknown Buddhist Stories in an Arabic Version* (London: Cassirer, 1971), p. 1.
41. *Ibid.*
42. *Ibid.,* p. 33.
43. *India and Christendom,* pp. 84-99. Garbe builds upon the previous work of M. Gaster and J. S. Speyer.
44. *Ibid.,* p. 89. See *Jataka,* no. 12.
45. *Ibid.,* p. 92.

46. After learning how effective elephants could be in battle against cavalry, the Greeks and Romans were quick to borrow this mode of warfare from India. Within a few years the most desired gift among Western kings probably was an Indian war elephant complete with an Indian mahout. Unfortunately for the Mediterranean generals, the African species of elephants were not so trainable and therefore not nearly so helpful in war.
47. Garbe, *India and Christendom,* pp. 99-108.
48. See, e.g., the footnotes concerning Christian art parallels to the life of the Buddha according to sutta no. 123 in the Majjhima-nikāya, in Karl Eugen Neumann, *Die Reden Gotamo Buddho's Mijjhimanikāyo,* pp. 700-709. For the Buddhist art of the Jatakas, see, e.g., S. F. Oldenburg, "Notes on Buddhist Art," *Journal of the American Oriental Society,* XVIII, 183-201. For illustrations of more modern Buddhist Jataka art, see E. Wray, *et al., Ten Lives of the Buddha: Siamese Temple Paintings and Jataka Tales* (New York: Weatherhill, 1972). The Wray book includes the story and illustrations of Vishvantara (Vessantara in Pali spelling).
49. R. A. Jairazbhoy, *Oriental Influences in Western Art* (Bombay: Asian Publishing House, 1965).
50. The Sanskrit word *japa* means something "repeated quietly," or murmured, for example, "a prayer." The second part of the compound, *mālā,* means "garland" and is often compounded with the names of flowers. So *japamālā* means "prayer-garland." However, if the second *a* of the word *japa* is long it becomes one of the words for "rose." I would add to the argument the point that in some of the Northwest Indian dialects the distinction between the short and broad vowels was lessened, making the words for prayer-garland and for rose-garland near homonyms. Given the usual association of the word garland with flowers, "rose-garland" is an understandable though mistaken translation.
51. See the discussion in Garbe, *India and Christendom,* pp. 119-20.
52. E.g., see Bernard Cooke, *Ministry to Word and Sacraments: History and Theology* (Philadelphia: Fortress Press, 1976).
53. William E. Phipps, "Did Ancient Indian Celibacy Influence Christianity?" *Studies in Religion,* 1974–75, pp. 45-50.
54. See Ernst Benz, "Indische Einflüsse auf die frühchristliche Theologie," *Akademie der Wissenschaften und der Literatur: Abhandlungen der Geistes—und Sozialwissenschaftlichen Klasse,* 1951, no. 3.
55. *Ibid.,* p. 202.
56. *Ibid.,* p. 197.
57. An important archaeological discovery was the uncovering of an ancient Coptic library at Nag Hammadi, Egypt, in 1945. The library contained non-Christian and Christian writings, including writings ascribed to John, James, Paul, and Peter, along with the Gospel of Thomas, a book of sayings attributed to Jesus.
58. There are two apocryphal gospels ascribed to Thomas. One is a gospel of

Jesus' infancy and childhood, which I am calling the "infancy Gospel of Thomas." The other consists of over a hundred sayings of Jesus, with no narrative, and was not extant until the uncovering of the Nag Hammadi Library of ancient Egypt.
59. That is, discourse number 123 of the *Middle Length Sayings.*
60. Neumann, *Die Reden Gotamo Buddho's Majjhimanikāyo,* iii.702 (footnote 115).
61. Cited from Al-Ghazali in Joachim Jeremias, *Unknown Sayings of Jesus* (London: S.P.C.K., 1964), pp. 114-15.
62. See Itivuttaka no. 100, Sutta-nipāta no. 560 for examples. The epithet is also found in the biographies such as the Lalita-vistara.
63. Cited from the Visuddhimagga by Nyanatiloka, *Buddhist Dictionary* (Colombo: Island Hermitage Publications, 1956), p. 140.
64. Gradual Sayings, i.60. Perhaps both the Buddhist and Christian mentionings of angels on pinpoints derives from a common Iranian influence, for angelology seems to have its origin in Iran.
65. The book mentions a bird called *charadrios* that can carry a person's illness to the sun, which consumes the disease. Garbe *(India and Christendom,* p. 66) notes that this must surely be related to the bird called *haridrava* in ancient Indian books (Rigveda 1.50.12; Atharvaveda 1.22.4) for this bird with a similar name carries away jaundice, to the sun it would seem.
66. The *Physiologus* reports that elephants have no bendable joints at the knees and so cannot get back up if they should ever fall. It adds that the Indians—a specific reference to India—take advantage of this and capture them by partially sawing through a tree trunk and then capturing the elephant when it leans against the tree to sleep. This is similar to an Indian story that tells about some hunters who capture a rhinoceros by seizing it before it can recover from falling after leaning against a rotten tree to sleep.
67. See Garbe, *India and Christendom,* p. 61-66.
68. This reflects a common belief in ancient India that an ascetic, especially a hermit, built up in himself tremendous psychic power (*tapas,* "heat") as a result of his meritorious practices.
69. Edward Conze, "Buddhism and Gnosis," *Le Origini dello Gnosticismo* (Leiden: Supplements to NUMEN, 1967), p. 656.

Chapter 4. A Case for Buddhist Influence

1. For a good recent discussion of the Q source, see Richard A. Edwards, *A Theology of Q* (Philadelphia: Westminster Press, 1975).
2. See the clear summary of the nature of Q and the positions taken concerning it in Howard Clarke Kee, *Jesus in History: An Approach to the Study of the Gospels* (New York: Harcourt, Brace and World, 1970), chapter 3, pp. 62-103. Kee finds eleven passages of eschatological warning, three on eschatological conflict, seven on eschatological promise, and so forth.

3. This incident is related in the Pali biography (Intro. to the Jatakas).
4. I have translated the second half of verse 168 according to the way the verse appears in the Pali Dhammapada, following Brough's suggestion that the text he edited has a scribal error at this point: What I translate as "angels" are in the original named "the shining gods."
5. The text uses the word *ptōchoi* rather than *penēs*.
6. If the Buddhist verses do lie behind the Q source at this point, however, we can speculate that Luke's first two blessings correspond to the Dharmapada couplet 167-68, and the second two correspond to couplet 165-66 (as I have cited them). Matthew's version is even more removed from the Buddhist parallels. Matthew's longer list of beatitudes includes verses influenced directly by Old Testament passages (Isa. 61:2, 60:21; Ps. 37:11), and Matthew rearranges the Lucan order.
7. Although the Pali and Gandhari versions of this saying are practically identical, the two recensions do use different verbs. The Pali *avekkheyya* means, "look down upon," "consider"; and the Gandhari *samikse'a* means "desire to see," "perceive," or in this case perhaps "investigate."
8. The dictionary definitions of *krino* include "separate," "distinguish," "judge," "consider," "look upon," "decide." William F. Arndt and F. Wilbur Gingrich, *A Greek-English Lexicon of the New Testament and Other Early Christian Literature* (Chicago: University of Chicago Press, 1957), p. 452.
9. In his effort to relate nearly all the Q sayings to an eschatological message, Howard Kee *(Jesus in History,* p. 77) sees this passage as an eschatological warning. But in this case the interpretation seems a bit foreign to the sayings themselves, for they seem more concerned with discouraging the practice of judging than with the End of the current era.
10. There is a possibility that the Buddhist passage refers to bamboo rather than thorns. The difference in the Sanskrit spelling for the word for thorn and one of the words for bamboo is very slight, which has led to confusion among Buddhist commentators and translators. See John Brough, ed., *The Gāndhārī Dharmapada* (London: Oxford University Press, 1962), p. 245, for the evidence in favor of the meaning "bamboo." Whatever the original meaning in the Indian languages, it is quite possible that the word came into Western languages as "thorn," rightly or wrongly.
11. The word *sapron* began with the meaning "rotten," but in Greek usage in the New Testament era had taken on the general meaning "bad," in the sense of unusable. For example, in the building trade unusable or crumbly stones could be called *sapron*. So the word is well suited to its context here, where it means rotten fruit in particular and bad in general.
12. The Buddhist parallels for verses 43 and 45 are less striking and come from other parts of the GDh. If verse 44 has been influenced by the Buddhist verse, then we must imagine Luke or his source constructing the striking opening sentence about good versus bad fruit trees in order to set the

context of the teaching, and constructing verse 45 to make clear the human application of the simile. However, Matt. 12:33-35 is similar enough to verses 43 and 45 to raise the possibility that some form of these verses existed in the Q source.
13. The term, in Sanskrit spelling, is *rāga,* which is often translated as "lust" or "passion," but I give the broader meaning "evil desires" to avoid giving the mistaken impression that the passage refers exclusively to sexual improprieties.
14. Franklin Edgerton translates the verb used as "shatters" in his *Buddhist Hybrid Sanskrit Grammar and Dictionary* (Delhi: Motilal Banarsidass, 1972).
15. Luke uses the word "river" in the singular, calling up the image of a river near the house which overflows and causes the house to fall. Matthew uses the plural form "rivers," which suggests the "mountain torrents or winter torrents which arise in ravines after a heavy rain and carry everything before them." (Arndt and Gingrich, *Greek-English Lexicon, "potamos,"* p. 701.) The reader should also note that the Buddhist text describes the poorly built house first. I have cited verse 220 before 219 to place them opposite their biblical parallels.
16. Paul Hanly Furtey, "Christ as Tekton," *The Catholic Biblical Quarterly,* April, 1955, p. 206.
17. I refer to Luke's account of the lowering of the paralytic through a roof. See the discussion in Kee, *Jesus in History,* p. 65.
18. See Nānamoli, *Life of the Buddha* (Kandy: Buddhist Publication Society, 1972), p. 317.
19. Some early Greek manuscripts have seventy, others seventy-two. Either number can be interpreted as a symbol for all of the nations of the world.
20. Nānamoli, *Life of the Buddha,* p. 52.
21. *The Dhammapada* (London: Oxford University Press, 1950), p. 180.
22. Compare GDh 2 and Uv 33.8.
23. Actually the story of the man with the barns does not occur in Matthew, so it is not from Q according to the definition of that source that I have been using. I mention the story at this point, however, because there is a group of sayings on heavenly treasure in Luke 12, some of which Matthew also employs and some of which he does not.
24. The Buddhist passage cited is from the Udanavarga and is not found in the Pali Dhammapada or the Gandhari Dharmapada. (However, it is in the "Faith" chapter of the Udanavarga, which is presumably among the lost chapters of the Gandhari version.) This means that on textual grounds it could be argued that the Buddhist parallel is post-Christian, with the Buddhists borrowing from the Christians in this case. However, the theme of the Buddhist passage is so common in other Buddhist texts that it seems likely the verse is original to Buddhism.
25. For more details see Amore, "The Concept and Practice of Doing Merit in

Early Theravada Buddhism" (dissertation, Columbia University, 1970), pp. 9-18.
26. The Tibetan version of the Udanavarga has "strive after *seclusion*" instead of wisdom. The Gandhari text is missing this verse, but it probably occurred in the lost chapters.
27. See Arndt and Gingrich, *Greek-English Lexicon,* under "mammon."
28. Perhaps the added reference to the prophetess Anna is a garbled version of the mention of Asita's nephew Nalada which concludes the Asita story, but if so I will be the first to admit how unlike the original it is. At least, such a theory would explain the presence of Anna in the story, since her role is so minimal that it is difficult to see why Luke bothered to mention her at all.
29. Cited from Edward J. Thomas, *The Life of Buddha as Legend and History* (London: Kegan Paul, Trench, Trubner & Co., 1927), pp. 53-54.
30. See Albert J. Edmund's article in *Open Court,* 1914, pp. 288 ff., and his article, "The Buddhist Origin of Luke's Penitent Thief," in the *Harvard Theologial Review* of 1914.
31. "The Provenance of Matthew's Gospel," *Studies in Religion,* 1973–74, pp. 220-35.
32. I do not agree that the number six is especially Buddhist, nor do I consider the passages on plucking out one's eye as at all parallel in meaning (and the book the Buddhist text occurs in, *Psalms of the Sisters,* may not have been known to the Middle Eastern Buddhists). The saying "Take my yoke upon you . . ." (Matt. 11:29-30) caused Osborne to speculate about a possible influence of the Indian word *yoga* upon the Greek word for yoke (*zugon*). (He points out that both words would have been pronounced the same way, a claim that I have no way of evaluating.) I am not willing to accept this as an example of influence because the passage makes good sense when *zugon* is taken in its usual sense of yoke. *Zugon* and *yoga* are so much alike because they are cognate terms in cousin languages, Greek and Sanskrit. Also, I find no parallel to this text. As for the "treasures in heaven" passage, I accept this as very likely to have been influenced by Buddhism, as I have already discussed.
33. Van den Bergh first called attention to this passage in the Gospel of Hebrews and argued for Buddhist influence upon it.
34. G. D. Kilpatrick, *The Origins of the Gospel According to St. Matthew* (London: Oxford University Press, 1950), p. 23.
35. The two verses are found together only in the Pali Dhammapada, not in the Gandhara or Udanavarga versions.
36. See Beal, *The Romantic Legend of Sākya Buddha* (London: Trubner & Co., 1875), p. 383.
37. *Ibid.,* p. 302.
38. Cited from Radhakrishnan, *Eastern Religions and Western Thought* (London: Oxford University Press, 1940), p. 180.
39. See the article "Money" in the *Interpreter's Dictionary of the Bible.*

40. The Sutralankara by Asvaghosa, which is post-Christian. I am following the version given in Samuel Beal, *Abstract of Four Lectures on Buddhist Literature in China,* (London: Trubner & Co., 1882), pp. 170-72.
41. J. Edgar Bruns, *The Christian Buddhism of St. John* (New York: Paulist Press, 1971), p. vii.
42. The Buddhist story is found in the fifth sutra of the *Middle Length Sayings.* See Edmunds' parallel number 36.
43. The story of the physician who cured a blind man and then discussed the karmi cause of blindness occurs in the Lotus Sutra and is usually singled out as the Buddhist parallel here.
44. Heinz Röhr, "Buddha und Jesus in ihren Gleichnissen," *Neue Zeitschrift für Systematische Theologie und Religionsphilosophie,* 15.65-86.
45. *Kindred Sayings,* trans. Mrs. Rhys Davids and F. L. Woodward (London: Pali Text Society, 1919–), i.23.
46. J. Edgar Bruns, "Ananda: The Fourth Evangelist's Model for 'the disciple whom Jesus loved'?" *Studies in Religion,* 1973–74, pp. 236-43.
47. According to Max Müller, as cited by Bruns, "Ananda," footnote 21.
48. Cited from Thomas, *Life of Buddha,* p. 243.
49. *Ibid.*

Cover design and art by Alene Moran. Interpretation of Jesus based on an eleventh-century Roman painting of the Last Judgment, signed "Johannes" and "Nicolaus," now in the Vatican. Interpretation of the Buddha based on the eighth-century Hokke Mandala representation of the Sakyamuni Buddha (Chinese or Japanese; Boston Museum).

BIBLIOGRAPHY OF PRINCIPAL SOURCES USED

Biographies of the Buddha

Abhiniskramanasūtra, trans. from Chinese by Samuel Beal, as *The Romantic Legend of Sākya Buddha*. London: Trubner & Co., 1875.

Lalita Vistara, trans. P. E. Foucaux as *Le Lalita Vistara*. Paris: Annales du Musée Guimet, 1884.

Mahāvastu, trans. J. J. Jones as *The Mahāvastu. Sacred Books of the Buddhists,* vols. xv-xvii. London: Luzac and Co., 1952.

Nidānakathā, trans. T. W. Rhys Davids in *Buddhist Birth Stories*. London: Routledge, n.d.

Versions of the Dharmapada

Dhammapada, trans. Irving Babbitt as *The Dhammapada*. New York: New Directions, 1965. (And many other English translations.)

The Gāndhāri Dharmapada, ed. John Brough. London: Oxford University Press, 1962.

Udānavarga, trans. W. Woodville Rockhill. London: Kegan Paul, Trench, Trubner & Co., 1892.

Other texts

The Book of the Discipline, 6 vols. Trans. I. B. Horner, *Sacred Books of the Buddhists*. London: Luzac, 1952–72.

The Book of the Gradual Sayings (Anguttara-Nikāya), 4 vols. Trans. F. L. Woodward and E. M. Hare. London: Pali Text Society, 1961–70.

The Book of Kindred Sayings (Samyutta-Nikāya), 5 vols. Trans.

Mrs. Rhys Davids and F. L. Woodward. London: The Pali Text Society, 1952–71.

The Collection of Middle Length Sayings (Majjhima-Nikāya), 3 vols. Trans. I. B. Horner. London: Pali Text Society, 1967–70.

Dialogues of the Buddha (Dīgha-Nikāya), 4 vols. Trans. T. W. and C. A. F. Rhys Davids, *Sacred Books of the Buddhists.* London: Luzac, 1969–77.

The Jātaka; or Stories of the Buddha's Former Births, 6 vols. ed. E. B. Cowell. London: Pali Text Society, 1973.

Saddharma-Pundarīka: or The Lotus of the True Law. Trans. H. Kern. New York: Dover Publications, 1963.

Sutta-Nipāta. Trans. V. Fausboll. Oxford, *Sacred Books of the East,* vol. x, 1881.

INDEX

INDEX OF SCRIPTURE REFERENCES

See also Index of Subjects for listings of entire works.

Hebrew
Genesis 2 16
Deuteronomy 35
Psalms 35
Isaiah 66:17 108
Daniel 108
Enoch 107-8
4 Ezra 108

Christian
Matthew
2:1-12 160-61
3:13-17 161
4:1-11 139
5:3-11 69
5:13 79
5:14-16 78
5:22 161
5:27-29 65
6:19-21 71
6:19-34 149
6:22-23 .... 78, 148
6:24 .... 151, 180
6:25-34 .... 68, 152, 180-81
6:47-49 79-80
7:1-6 .... 66, 162
7:6 76-77
7:13-14 162
7:15 .... 75, 163
7:16-20 .... 75, 76
8:18-19 146
8:18-22 117
8:19-22 .... 43, 44
12:33-35 144
13:44 74
14:28-33 .... 93, 163
15:17-20 42
17:1-2 146
17:1-8 46
17:20 .... 94, 164
24:14 .... 46, 164
25:14-30 164
26:6-13 156
27:51-52 49

Mark
1:12-13 .... 32-33, 139
4:3-8 .... 80-81, 165
4:14-20 .... 80-81, 165
4:26-29 .... 82, 165
6:18-23 168
6:45-52 166-67
8:22-26 87
10:17-25 72
12:41-44 168-69
14:3-9 156

Luke
1:26-38 153
2:6-7 154
2:8-14 .... 154, 179
2:10-13 .... 24, 116
2:21-24 .... 155, 179
2:25-35 .... 26, 27, 179
3:21-22 32
4:1-13 .... 33, 34, 139, 179

Index of Scripture References

4:18-19 .... 88, 97
4:29 41
6:17 59
6:20-49 .... 69, 140-41, 179
6:27-37 .... 61-62, 141, 179
6:39 .... 67, 179
6:40 142
6:41-42 14-43
6:43-45 .... 75, 76, 144, 179
6:46-49 .... 79-80, 145, 179
7:35-50 .... 156, 179
7:38 .... 51, 179
9:28-29 .... 146, 179
9:57-62 .... 146, 179
10:1-11 .... 44, 45, 179
10:19 147
11:27-28 156
11:34-35 .... 148, 179
11:37-39 .... 149, 179
12:13-21 156
12:15-21 150
12:16-21 .... 71, 72, 179
12:22-31 .... 149, 179
12:32-34 .... 71, 150, 179
12:33 179
13:23-24 162
15:2 85
15:11-32 .... 83, 157, 179
16:13 .... 151, 179
16:19-31 72
21:1-4 .... 168, 169

John
1:48 172
4:7, 9-10, 13-15 .... 40, 41
6:60-65 172
7:38 .... 92, 102
10:17-18 49
12:34 .... 49, 102

James 3:6 .... 103, 176

I Peter 3:19 175

II Peter 3:10-12 175

James 131-32

Hebrews 16

Buddhist

Theravada (Pali)

Dharmapada (Gāndhāri)
1-2 .... 75, 19
139 70
164 74
165-67 141
165-68 179
169 141
180 61
201-2 144
219-20 .... 79, 145, 179
221-22 162
226 68
258 .... 75, 143, 179
264 162
270 65
271-72 .. 179, 66, 142-43, 162
273 76-77
280-81 .... 179, 61-62, 141
283 63
303-4 78

Dhammapada (Pali)
1-2 144
3-5 61
13-14 79
50 151
75 66
83 68
87 117
91-92 .... 43-44, 179
92-93 .... 68, 149, 179
155 70
163 162
201 61
219-20 70
244-45 162

252	66
290	74
309	65
394	75, 149

Jātaka Stories
  no. 12 122-23
  no. 78 .... 89, 103
  no. 190 .... 93, 103
  no. 526 134

Sutta-Nipāta
  no. 32 34
  no. 241 168
  no. 242 42
  no. 806 72

Other

Udanavarga
  1.20-22 ...... 71-72, 150, 179

5.23	70
8.8	144
9.7	67, 179
9.8	76
10.11	71, 179
13.1	181
13.5	179, 180
13.6	151, 180
13.7-10	180
22.5	78, 179
27.2-3	162
27.5	78, 148, 179
28.16	162
29.11-12	75
30.33	74
32.1	68
33.13	42
33.45-46	61
33.68	65

INDEX OF AUTHORS

Bruns, Edgar, 169-71, 173-74
Conze, Edward, 135
de Bunsen, Ernest, 97-98
Edmunds, Albert, 14, 99-102
Gandhi, Mahatma, 64
Garbe, Richard, 14, 102-4, 123, 166
Goddard, Dwight, 104
Jairazbhoy, R. A., 126
Kee, Howard, 138
Lillie, Arthur, 99
Neusner, Jacob, 108-10
Notovitch, Nicolas, 114-15
Osborne, Robert E., 160
Pfleiderer, Otto, 98-99
Radhakrishnan, S., 104-5
Röhr, Heinz, 173
Schmiedel, Otto, 99
Seydel, R., 98, 172
Thomas, Edward, 105
Valée Poussin, Louis de la, 105
Van Eysinga, van den Bergh, 98

INDEX OF SUBJECTS

Adultery, 168
Ammonius Sakkas, 128-29
Ananda, 40, 173-74
Angel-messiah, Christ as, 97.
  See also Jesus Christ
Angels, 23-24, 107, 153
Anger, 59-64

Arahants, 44
Architecture, religious, 125
Art. *See* Buddhist art
Aryans, 16
Ascension, 50
Ashoka, 112
Asita, 26, 28, 102-3, 155

Index of Subjects

Astrology, 28
Avatar. *See* God in human body

Barlaam and Josaphat, saints, 119-20
Bhikkhus, 44
Blindness to social status, 39
Boddhisattva (Bodhisat), 18, 26-27, 120. *See also* Bodily signs; Gautama Buddha
Bodily signs, of greatness, 25
Brahma (god), 17
Buddha. *See* Gautama Buddha
Buddhist art, 125-26, 132
Buddhist influence on Christianity
 in apocryphal gospels, 114-15, 129-33
 in art (*see* Buddhist art)
 in New Testament, 137-86
 in physiologus, 134-36
 possibility of, 106-36
 in matters of ritual and dress, 126-27
 history of scholarship on, 96-105, 128-29, 160, 166, 169-76
 in stories of saints, 119-25
 See also Parallels, Buddhist and Christian

Celibacy, 128
Christopher, Saint, 124
Church, Christian, 46, 53
Confession, 127
Contentedness, 67-69, 140-41
Cosmic events at death of master, 29, 49-50, 164

Death, conquering, 48-49
Detachment, 132-33. *See also* Homelessness; Contentedness; Lust, avoidance of; Possessions.
Devil (Mara, Satan), 32-37, 48, 103
Dhamayanti and Nala, story of, 16

Dharmaguptaka sect, 113
Dharmapada (Dhammapada), 11-12, 59, 113. *See also Buddhist section in Index of Scripture References*
Dialogues of the Buddha, 46-47, 49, 179
Disciples, 39, 42-46
Discipline, Book of the, 41, 43-45, 92, 179
Divinity of master. *See* Veneration of masters
Divyāvadāna, 40-41
Docetic heresy, 20

Elijah, 46-47
Enlightenment, 30-31, 38, 47. *See also* Gautama Buddha
Eschaton, 138
Essenes. *See* Qumran community
Eustace legend, 122

Feet of master, revered by woman, 51-52, 179
Finger-garland. *See* Thief, conversion of
Forgiveness, 47, 57
Four Noble Truths, 133. *See also* Gautama Buddha, teachings of

Ganges Spirituality, 11, 20, 60, 141
Gatha verses, 59, 85
Gautama Buddha
 ascension of, 50
 preaching begun, 38
 birth of, 12, 22-25, 152
 childhood of, 18-31, 154-55, 161
 conception of, 21-22
 deification of, 20
 descent of, 15
 quest for enlightenment by, 30-31, 38, 47
 return to heaven, 17, 45
 transfiguration of, 46-47, 146
 veneration of, 51
 See also God in human body

205

Gautama Buddha, teachings of
  contentment, 67-68
  disciples, 39-45
  forgiveness, 48
  homelessness, 53, 133
  lust, avoidance of, 65, 162
  money matters, 45
  nonviolence, 41
  personal defilement, 60-62
  pure mind, 58
  purity, spiritual, 41-42
  sharing wealth, 73
  similarities with Jesus' teaching, 13 (*see also* Parallels, Christian and Buddhist)
  social harmony, 41
  temptation, 32-35, 139
  theme of disciplined disciple, 77-78
Gnosticism, 135, 169-70
God, 36, 38. *See also* God in human body, God in spiritual body
Goddess of Wisdom, 135
God in human body (avatar), 16, 54-57, 97. *See also* Ascension
God in spiritual body, 16, 20-21, 54-57
Gradual Sayings, Book of the, 43, 82-83, 94, 131, 133
Hadrian, 123
Hatred. *See* Anger
Heaven. *See* Treasures in heaven
Hell, 65-66
Hellenism, 108-9. *See also* Gnosticism
Herod, 30
Homelessness, 50, 78, 116, 132-33, 146
Hydaspes River, 123

Immortality, 48-49. *See also* Treasures in heaven
Incarnation, 55-58
Iran, 107-8, 160-61

Jātaka, Introduction to, 24, 26-27, 139, 156, 175, 179

Jesus Christ
  baptism by John, 32, 161
  birth of, 12, 22-25, 153-54
  childhood of, 25-29, 154-55, 160-61
  conception of, 21-22
  decision to preach, 38
  deification of, 20
  descent of, 15
  enlightenment, 30-31, 38, 47
  fasting and spiritual searching, 33
  forgiveness, 48
  homeless life-style of, 39, 116
  last years of, 114-15
  return to heaven, 45, 50, 55
  temptation of, 32-35, 139
  transfiguration of, 46-47, 146-47
  veneration of, 51
  See also God in human body; Parallels, Buddhist and Christian
Jesus Christ, teachings of
  Buddhist influence upon (*see* Buddhist influence on Christianity)
  contentment, 67-68, 140-41
  discipline, 77-78
  forgiveness, 48, 141
  homelessness, 43, 53, 116-17, 132-33
  instructing disciples, 42-43, 147-52
  interpretations of tradition, 41
  money matters, 45, 73
  nonviolence, 61-62
  purity, spiritual, 41-42, 58
  sexual matters, 53, 65, 161
  similarities with Buddhism (*see* Parallels, Buddhist and Christian)
Jesus' baptism. *See* Jesus Christ
Jewels, Three Precious (Triple Gem) of Buddhism, 46
John the Baptist, 38, 97, 117, 152
Josaphat, Saint. *See* Barlaam and Josaphat, saints

Index of Subjects

Judgmental state of mind, 66-67, 142, 162

Karma, 60, 65-67, 69-70, 144. *See also* Merit
Kassapa, 92, 167
Kindred Sayings, Book of the, 80-82, 173
Krishna tradition, 20

Lalita Vistara, 29, 98, 130
Legendary pattern, 15-18, 21, 27-28
Levitation, miracle of, 90, 92-93, 163, 166
Light of the world, 74, 148, 179
Lotus Sutra, 83-84, 157, 174-75, 179
Love of enemies, 141
Lust, avoidance of, 65

Magi, 27-29, 160-61
Mahāparinibbāna Sutta. *See* Dialogues of the Buddha
Mahāvamsa, 21
Mahāvastu, 36, 87-88, 92, 179
Mahayana Buddhism, 170-71
  deification of Buddha, 51
Mammon. *See* Possessions
Mara. *See* Devil
Mary
  compared to Maya, 131-32
  Simeon's words to, 27
  as virgin, 15, 22-24, 152-53
Maya
  compared to Mary, 131-32
  death of, 25
  as mother of Buddha, 15, 22-24, 29
Merit, 35, 69. *See also* Karma
Middle Length Sayings, 131
Miracles
  faith-inducing, 90-94, 167
  healing, 86-88
  multiplication, 88-89, 166
  in nature, 90
  purpose of, 85-86, 95

Monasticism, 53, 126-27. *See also* Homelessness, Bhikkhus
Money, 45. *See also* Possessions
Monks, Buddhist. *See* Bhikkhus
Mother of master, blessed, 157

Nagas (divine cobras), 129
Namuci. *See* Devil
New Testament. *See Index of Scripture References*
Nirvana
  not like heaven, 19, 50-51, 74
  as ultimate liberation, 50, 151
Nonviolence
  taught by masters, 49-63
  for social reform, 64, 112

Parables, 71, 80-85, 145, 165-66
Parallels, Buddhist and Christian
  birth and childhood, 21-24, 129-30, 152-54, 160-61, 179
  contentedness, 66-68, 179-81
  death, 49-50
  devil, 48
  disciples, 42-43, 173-74, 179
  divinity of master, 51
  forgiveness, 47, 179
  hell, 63, 161, 179
  homelessness, 43-44, 132-33, 179-80
  God in human body, 56
  kings visit infant master, 27-29, 160-61
  lust, avoidance of, 65
  miracles, 85-95, 163-64, 166-67
  money matters, 45-46, 73, 151, 168-69, 179-80
  moral pragmatism, 76
  nonviolence, 60-62
  parables, 80-85, 157-58, 165-66, 179
  prophecy, 26, 102-3, 155, 175
  pure mind, 58

Parallels, Buddhist and Christian *(continued)*
  sacrifice, 56
  social status unimportant, 39-41
  spiritual purity, 41-42
  star at birth of master, 28
  teachings, 58-79, 141-52, 159-77
  temptation of master, 34-38, 179
  transfiguration, 46-47, 146-47, 179
  treasures in heaven (merit), 71, 150-51, 179
  veneration of master, 51, 55, 179
Persian influence. *See* Iran
Peter, 93, 163
Pharisees, 149
Physiologus, 134
Possessions, 151-52. *See also* Treasures in heaven
Power, spiritual, 87, 94. *See also* Merit, Miracles
Prajña, 135
Prajñaparamita, 135
Prodigal son, parable of, 83-84, 157, 179
Pure mind, 58, 80

Qumran community, 97, 106-7, 117, 173
Q Source, 137-52, 164-65, 178-84

Rebirth, wheel of, 176
Reincarnation, 128, 176
Repentance, 45
Ritual, 127-29
Rosary, 127

Sacrifice, animal, 57
Saints. *See* Arahants, Barlaam and Josaphat, Christopher
Samadhi, 94
Samsara. *See* Reincarnation
Sangha, 46

Satan. *See* Devil
Sermon on the Mount, 11-12, 59, 64, 140-46, 152
Sermon on the Plain, 59. *See also* Sermon on the Mount
Sexual intercourse
  avoided by mothers of masters, 22, 152-53
  incompatible with holiness, 22
  masters coneived without, 15, 18-19, 22
  See also Lust
Siddhartha, 25. *See also* Gautama Buddha
Simeon, the sage, 26-27, 102-3, 155
Sinhalese race, 21
Social status, unimportance of, 43-46
Star at masters' births, 28
Staveravada (Theravada) sect of Buddhism, 113
Stupa (thupa), 55
Suddhodana, King, 24
Sutasoma, Prince, 124

Temptation, 32-38, 139-40. *See also* God in human body
Thief, conversion of, 48, 92-93, 158
Transmigration, 128
Treasures in heaven, 69-74, 151-52
Turbo, Marcius, 123

Veneration of masters, 51-52, 55
Vishnu Hinduism 20. *See also* Krishna tradition
Vishvantara, King, 125

Woman at the well, 39-44, 172
Woman with two coins, 168-69

Zen Buddhism, 12
Zoroastrianism, 107, 160. *See also* Iran